THE
DESIGNER'S WORKSPACE:
ULTIMATE OFFICE DESIGN

THE
DESIGNER'S WORKSPACE:
ULTIMATE OFFICE DESIGN

Douglas B. Caywood, Associate AIA, CSI, CDT

AMSTERDAM • BOSTON • HEIDELBERG • LONDON • NEW YORK • OXFORD
PARIS • SAN DIEGO • SAN FRANCISCO • SINGAPORE • SYDNEY • TOKYO

Architectural Press is an imprint of Elsevier

ELSEVIER

Architectural
Press

Architectural Press
An imprint of Elsevier
Linacre House, Jordan Hill, Oxford OX2 8DP
200 Wheeler Road, Burlington MA 01803

First published 2004

British Library Cataloguing in Publication Data

Library of Congress Cataloguing in Publication Data
A catalogue record for this book is available from the Library of Congress

ISBN 0 7506 5739 1

For information on all Architectural Press publications
visit our website at www.architecturalpress.com

Typeset by Keyword Typesetting Services, Wallington, Surrey
Printed and bound in Italy

Table of Contents

Ross/Fowler Lobby

Ross/Fowler Gallery

Ross/Fowler Large Conference

Ross/Fowler Studio Layout

Ross/Fowler Small Conference

Acknowledgements

From a mere idea stated during the programming stage of our own offices to the release of the final manuscript, there have been so many individuals and institutions I would like to thank for their support and/or encouragement.

Alison Yates and Elizabeth Whiting, for their continued support and help in establishing the contracts, approval of this endeavor, answering of numerous questions, and reviews of material; Ross/Fowler, P.C. – Charles Ross II, AIA and Mike Fowler, ASLA, for their support and establishment of the idea for this book during the move of our firm to a new location; Kathy Proctor, FCSI, CDT, for a review from the academia perspective; Andrew P. Powers, AIA, for a review from an architectural perspective; Danielle Culp Mathews for a review from an interior design perspective; contacts through the University of Tennessee College of Architecture and Design; Dean Marleen K. Davis at the University of Tennessee College of Architecture for her recommendations; David Smith, CDT for his involvement in graphic layout; Mark DeKay, for his advice from previous author/publisher agreements; Christy Lane for her assistance in mailings and firm correspondence; Jill Humberd for assistance in reviewing the final proofs; my parents, Donald and Nancy Caywood, for their patience and support during 2002; my family and friends for their continued encouragement; and to a long list of those who gave recommendations and provided submissions throughout this book.

I would like to thank each participating firm for the time, effort, and information that you have provided throughout this process. With minor editing, this book includes text and photo- graphy received from each firm, including firm description and concept statements. For layout and editing purposes, original text from each firm may have been manipulated with careful interpretation so as to not change intent by each firm. Each firm was given proofs for layout, text, and credits for their approval.

And, in conclusion, I would like to give praise and honor to God for the strength and time He has given me to produce this publication.

'I can do all things through
Christ who strengthens me.'
Philippians 4:13

Introduction

the designer's workspace

Is there an ultimate layout for a design professional's office? The likelihood of a designer answering yes to this question is quite high, but, with the variety of design solutions to follow, it is apparent that 'ultimate' takes on a very individualistic meaning for each firm.

While working in a firm that made the decision that we had outgrown the historic Ely building in downtown Knoxville, Tennessee, research began for a new location. What type of building were we searching for? Was our intention to attempt an adaptive reuse or renovation? How much new space was needed? What financial stipulations are involved? What image will the new design studio reveal about our design philosophy?

These are only a sample of the questions that ran through the minds of the staff of our firm. As the research and schematic design began, we found numerous resources on office design, the at-home office, and various other offices for different project types — what we did not find was an extensive technical and image resource that included only the offices of designers and what differentiates a designer's office from any other type of office. Throughout the world, architects and interior designers work each day on office designs for their clients. 'The Designer's Workspace: Ultimate Office Design' will begin to describe the unique attributes of a designer's office and feature various firms throughout the world and how they have solved the 'ultimate office' design opportunity.

ultimate office design

Ely Building
Knoxville, TN

First, we must decide who is the client for which our office is to be designed — our employees, our clients or our CPA? Do we use our office to market our design talents? Do we create a space that can help our employees do their job? In this case, should the goal be to inspire the designer — or be as efficient as possible.

With many different goals present, this can present a complex design problem for each firm.

From the first impressions at the reception area and lobby, to the appeal of the meeting areas, or the functionality and sleekness of the design studio itself, the designer's office can be quite unique in style, function, and character. This uniqueness is also exemplified as spaces and design solutions vary from culture to culture.

The imagery of a design firm begins with the first impressions a client has of the **lobby** and the **reception area**. First impressions are lasting impressions and are hard to overcome, thus the impact of a design firm begins as a client walks through the door. Who are your clients and how can you design for them?

Is the firm's graphic or logo prominently positioned? Is the entry space unique to the firm? Is the lobby spacious? Is the firm's image well articulated? Is it cutting-edge or timeless? Is it lighthearted or serious-minded? This list could be quite exhaustive as the client or a new recruit stores mental images and perceptions of the designer and the work the firm is producing. Are your clients very conservative or will they appreciate the firm's innovative use of materials, connections, lighting, etc? It is important for the firm to concentrate on who their target client audience may be now, as well as in the future.

This space may also be a prelude to an awards or **project display** showcasing the firm's recent achievements and/or current projects. This aspect of a firm's public area may be one of the key distinctions of a designer's office, in contrast to a typical business's lobby area, which may remain static. Designers are always designing — keeping ideas and images fresh.

This element of a design firm can be constantly evolving, as projects progress from the color rendering to the final photography of the completed project, to an award received for the design. Each firm can tell their life story in very unique ways through these displays. Through the rest of this book, you will see a large variety of ways in which projects are displayed and how the firm's space greets the visitor.

Meeting areas are also unique as the designer requires multiple forms of media for presentations. From a wall surface for displaying large format drawings to a surround sound video presentation of an animation, meeting areas may take on many different roles. Flexibility and hands-on-access to various forms of media are key in a designer's typical day. Not only are conference rooms needed for client presentations, but these rooms may also facilitate design charettes within the office, large format layout reviews, business/ marketing meetings, videoconferencing with national and/or international affiliations, consultant reviews, product presentations by vendors and manufacturers, cocktail or holiday parties, etc. In many cases, medium and large size firms require a variety of sizes of meeting areas, ranging from the two person critique area to a presentation space for a new client with a board of directors numbering twenty or more. Layout, lighting, power, communications, and food/beverage serving area flexibility differentiate a designer's meeting area from a typical conference room. Through the following chapters, conference area creativity will be evident, from the conference room with storefront windows to an area that opens up to the outside with a fourteen foot glass garage door. The conference room is no

longer a typical rectangular room with a table and chairs, but a designer's pallette for creative communication space accommodating varieties of people for a period of time.

Library – a collection of resource material? This term only begins to explain the varieties of reference material, layout space and storage capabilities for the resources included in a designer's office. In many typical offices, the largest piece of correspondence may be an 11 x 17 sheet of paper. For a designer, print media can range from an $8\frac{1}{2}$ x 11 sheet to a drawing four feet wide and twelve feet in length. Storage of these types of media can be integral pieces of the design solution, as design firms require quick access to large sets of drawings which range in size from 24" x 36" to 30" x 42". Various methods of storage-rolled, hanging, or large format filing drawers — may be used.

In a typical business, transmittals may be sent with a stack of folders, whereas in a designer's office, transmittals may come or go with product samples of large construction materials or fixtures, large wall racks displaying color selections, or even large mounted renderings. With these media types, the **layout spaces** and the product and sample **libraries** become very important elements in a design firm. Designers are constantly selecting and specifying products, of which hands-on interaction with so many of these selections is imperative. With a majority of products now showcased on websites, the designer has the advantage of browsing through products and colors, but for the final presentation to the client, physical samples of colors, textures, and fixtures still remain the most effective selling tool. The storage and display areas for these products tend to grow proportionally by size of firm.

Reception

Gallery

Meeting

The realization '… *that we were both clients and the designers*.' Dasic Architects

As for a more common definition of library, design firms will not only have product and sample 'libraries', but they will also feature a magazine and reference book library. Designers are visually oriented and most thrive on viewing the latest periodicals and design-related books. The library should be one of the most inspirational and relaxing elements of the designer's workspace. The images to follow will show similar, yet contrasting, ways of displaying the catalogs, binders, reference material, and periodicals and using these necessities as design elements.

While the **reception area**, the **meeting areas,** and the **library** include design elements that are specific to each firm and the profession, the **studio** and/or **design space** for the designer has key elements of originality. For the designer, the normal working environment is the studio, reminiscent of the college educational model. This space is key to inspiring the designer and facilitating his/her production of the product.

With twenty designers asked to design the optimal workspace, in all probability you would have at least twenty different designs. Studios vary tremendously between firms, depending on the firm organization, how project teams are assigned, the configuration of the space allocated, and various other considerations on a firm by firm basis. Needs also change with an employee's role within the firm — hand rendering, animations, model building, marketing, construction documents, specifications, all of the above… Does a typical workstation need to accommodate all of these roles, or is a workstation task specific? How much storage is needed at each station? How much layout space is needed?

Interestingly, the examples throughout this book are very similar in size for each workstation, but the arrangement, lighting, storage, and relationship between workstations vary tremendously by firm.

The designer's office typically includes oversized desks and layout space for drawings. The industry has changed in the last two decades from a manual drafting table to a computer station. With these changes, mobility has become a priority for tables, carts, and seating to make the design space most versatile.

Varying by firm, a studio may include the entire design staff, including the principal(s) of the firm, or management may be in individual offices. This decision, in many cases, is representative of the firm's philosophy of the project team, how the project team(s) operate, and the level of flexibility and potential growth that is expected in the long range business plan of the firm.

What products are available to accommodate these functions and flexibility? Are designers using manufactured products or custom fabricated units? Many offices reflect total custom design with each studio desk and storage unit. Storage units can become an overall design element that visually tie the studio together. While varying from firm to firm, two design directions can be distinguished among the examples. Many firms focus on the interior finishes and articulation of details and space while providing standard, functional desktops and workspaces. Other firms provide custom individual workstations that provide an additional layer of detail to the studio.

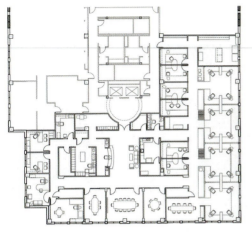

Ross/Fowler Office Layout

In the book – 'New Workplaces for New Workstyles' by Marilyn Zelinsky, the old rule of thumb is 250 square feet for individual offices, but offices have now decreased in size to 200 square feet and workstations to 80 square feet per person. These numbers are comparable to many of the design studio case studies as detailed to follow.

For many design professionals, the office becomes a 'home away from home' and is more than just a typical space for working. Many firms choose to offer additional amenities that revolve around break areas or some type of recreational activity. In many of the case studies, firms have incorporated the break areas with the library elements. Designers are very prone to browse through periodicals, books, or reference materials during breaks or at lunch. The minds of most design professionals are constantly turning with new ideas, which are fostered through interaction in the break areas and with frequent exposure to design product literature.

Imagine your lobby, your meeting areas, your library, your studio, your break areas . . . What do these images say about your firm to your employees, a visiting recruit, and your clients? Do these images give your client the best, lasting 'first impression'?

These descriptions of unique spaces that are incorporated into the designer's workspace are only a sample of the many design decisions and alternatives that may be explored during the design process. Our firm has had the opportunity to experience sixteen years in the three-story renovated Ely Building in downtown Knoxville, featuring an interior brick wall extending the full length of the building, large wooden windows lining each side of the studio, a conference room bay window, a sidewalk entrance with storefront, and other unique features of buildings from the turn of the 20th century.

Now the firm of twenty-one enjoys double the square footage on the third floor of a new office building located just one block away. There are many advantages to each of these offices. As we prepared the space to accommodate us and meet our needs, it gave us an opportunity to decide how to express the character and uniqueness of our firm.

Throughout the examples in this book, you will see the important elements for each firm and each firm's staff that influenced the final designs. After corresponding with hundreds of design firms for this publication, it was amazing to see the number of firms who did not consider their offices to be of publishable quality, but rather worked out of ordinary and non-descript offices. To the contrary, the examples in this book have stepped forward to display the unique and innovative solutions for their everyday design environments.

Has the ultimate design solution been achieved? This question can only be asked and answered individually by each firm. As each space of an office is dissected for its function, its image, and its quality of design, the professional has the distinct opportunity to make a lasting statement about the design firm. In observing your firm, how does your space characterize your firm's vision?

Studio

Office

Library

archimania

architecture

01

archimania™ is an architecture firm located in the downtown historic district of Memphis, Tennessee in a renovated 1,600 sf space originally built in 1910. The tenant space had been unoccupied in a neglected part of downtown. The design pallette was a dilapidated and empty shell space with worn plaster over masonry party walls, badly worn wood floors, and no mechanical, plumbing, or electrical systems.

The firm's goals were to design an office that was dramatic and impressive upon entry. Efficiency and open work and conference spaces were required for open communications in a small office. The firm promotes a strong teaching/learning environment for young employees and encouraged the use of cost effective material throughout the space.

The plaster ceilings were removed to expose the ceiling and roof joists, plaster walls were repaired and painted white, and the existing wood floors were salvaged in the public spaces of the office. Marine grade plywood was applied over the existing wood floors in the rear of the building and painted with a high gloss enamel.

date of completion	1996
number of employees	7
total square footage	1600
number of conference rooms	1
typical workspace size	64 sf

Photography Credits:
Jeffrey Jacobs/Arch. Photo. Inc.

3

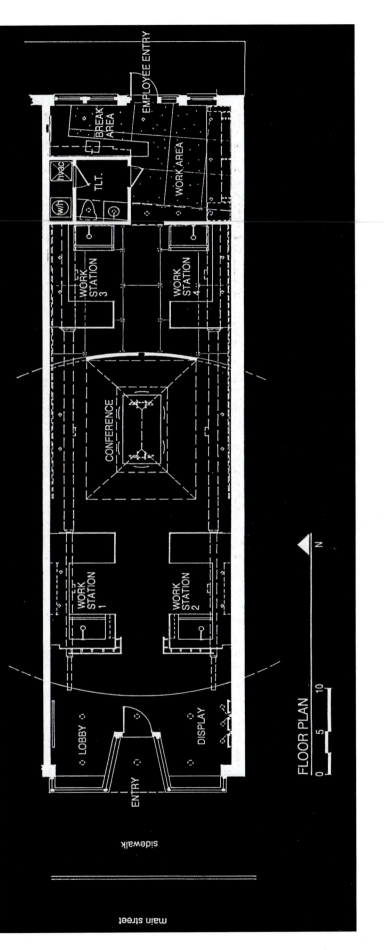

FLOOR PLAN

0   5   10

N

EMPLOYEE ENTRY

BREAK AREA

WORK AREA

hvac

TLT.

w/n

WORK STATION 3

WORK STATION 4

CONFERENCE

WORK STATION 1

WORK STATION 2

LOBBY

DISPLAY

ENTRY

sidewalk

main street

4

The skylight was re-trimmed and emphasized with a boldly painted curved wall as the backdrop. The skylight and curved wall serve as a focal point upon entry and the slot in the wall helps to express the implied symmetry of the office. The office is a series of layers manipulated by color, material, and form.

5

6 2

7

Architects Wells Kastner Schipper

1

02

Architects Wells Kastner Schipper – AWKS – is an architecture, planning, and interior design firm located in West Des Moines, Iowa. In the summer of 1998, this firm, previously Architects Wells Woodburn O'Neil, inhabited their new offices in an existing 1970's vintage public library. This was the departure point for this adaptive re-use project. The space is approximately one half of the previous public library. The windowless space had formerly housed a circulation desk and a stack area.

The design is based programmatically upon the firm's cultural expectations of open and informal communication, as well as providing clients a visual model of the firm's communicative culture, abilities in adaptive reuse, and design methodology based on simple expression of materials and their spatial relationships.

The first step in remodeling was the addition of light to the space. This was achieved by removing an entire wall of the building and replacing it with a curtain wall with fourteen feet of north faced vertical glass and one foot of horizontal glass at floor level at either end. The disengagement of the curtain wall from the existing floor and walls was the impetus for further study into treating the use of the space as temporary in the logic of its connections to the existing structure, while conveying strength and permanence to users and clientele. The curtain wall is aided structurally by a load bearing 'layout table' that is constructed of plate steel and limestone and the use of moment reducing tension rods.

The studio space is based around the 'studio table' which is the home for group discussions, supplies and printing devices. The table provides an opportunity for interaction by its central location and varied design-oriented uses. On axis with the 'studio table' is the 'office table.' Its use is related to non-design functions of mail, marketing, and filing. The personal interaction evoked by this table's use is similar to the 'studio table' and the relationship and difference of each table's activities are expressed through alignment and separation.

In keeping with expressions of open communication and often-temporal nature of adaptive re-use, doors are found only at the entrance to the space and the rest room. The wall and furnishing elements of the space do not engage the walls of the existing space and connections to the existing columns are limited to silicone engagements of glass. Material expressions emphasize the hearty and simplicity of wood, explore structural capabilities of steel in spans and tension, and highlight the varied properties of glass.

date of completion	1998
number of employees	17
total square footage	5500
number of conference rooms	2
typical workspace size	80 sf
custom workstations	yes

1 Curtain Wall
2 Floor Plan
3 Nightscape
4 Exterior

3

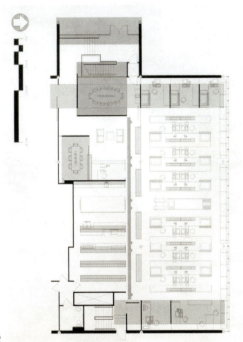

2

4

5

6

7

9

8

10

Augusto Quijano Arquitectos

1   2

03

Augusto Quijano Arquitectos, S. C. P. is an architecure firm located in Merida Yucatan Mexico. The firm's offices are designed with retranslated architectural elements from history, tradition, and fifteen years of practice. The use of space, natural lighting and history criteria were all key elements in the design process.

The building is closed to the street with 'vacuum' interiors. The scheme is organized with all spaces oriented around a hard-patio with a reflecting pool. There are two distinct spaces within the office – the working areas and the public areas. The service core links the two areas.

The design reflects the 'back spaces' such as portico, patio, backyard and zaguan (Mexican entry) as an attitude to claim tradition with place but spirit-of-age. The spatial organization uses a series of transition spaces with public-private sequences.

The interior language of the workspace is characterized by white, empty walls that are isolated planes that obtain fluency throughout the spaces. The design maintains a philosophy of spatial treatment and not from forms.

The firm's philosophy is reflected in the design of this workspace – 'The architecture is the mirror of the culture' and 'Culture is the way of life of people.'

3

date of completion	1992
number of employees	14
total square meters	178
number of conference rooms	3
typical workspace size	5 sqm

Photography Credits:
Augusto Quijano Axle Archive

4

5

10

11

Blue Sky Architecture

architecture

1

04

The studio has working stations for five architects, a conference area, a small kitchen area, lunch area and a washroom. As a home office, it allows for daytime occupancy in a neighborhood that is normally deserted during the business week and reduces commuting time for those involved in the office who live in the area. The construction budget was $96,000.

An addition to a modest West Coast Modern classic home of the sixties, this 900 sq. ft. studio knits between the existing house and a mature garden and pond. The studio flanks the east side of the property, forming a garden entrance courtyard between carpet and studio. The studio bridges across the slope tying into the existing structure.

The studio consists of a single open workspace. A large glass wall sweeps around the pond and garden, reaching towards the entrance on the public side of the property. The front curving wall rises with the same 3.5 in 12 roof slope as the existing house. A rafter and decking roof follows this rise, while resting on a constant ten foot high beam pulled free from the opposite wall. The roof appears to float, as the flanking wall is split from the roof by a continuous skylight that washes all of the shelving in natural light and balances the light in the space. Filtered light from the west comes through the mature cherry trees and rhododendrons and reflects from the pond.

2

date of completion	2000
number of employees	5
total square footage	900
number of conference rooms	1
typical workspace (average)	60 sf

1 Entry
2 Window Wall
3 Studio Entrance
4 Studio

hotography Credits:
Diego Samper 1, 2
Peter Powles 3, 4

3

4

Randy Brown Architects

1

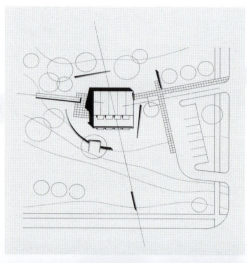

2

05

An environment for living and working — a studio/residence — this was the solution for Randy Brown Architects located in Omaha, Nebraska. The 40' x 40' 1970's passive solar building (originally a pre-school) and lot were purchased by the firm to be converted into a studio-residence. As an architectural experiment, the Architect decided to design and construct the project while living and working in the building. The only room that was designed and built before moving was the shower.

The existing building was stripped to its pure shell; the exterior is composed of white EIFS and the interior sheetrock walls have been painted white. The interior perimeter walls were intentionally left blank to provide maximum exhibit space for the studio's projects. The center of the building is occupied by a free-standing "platform/container"; a collage of pieces (bookcases, technology wall, closet, dresser, wall studs, floor joists, steel plates, retractable glass table) which create a communal space on the first floor and an office/sleeping loft above.

The initial answer to the problem was a studio/residence. By establishing only the final objective on which to base the projections, constructions, and intentions beforehand, a means remained to be discovered. An agenda secured with an ephemeral signature to ensure its security.

3

date of completion	1997
number of employees	4
total square footage	1,600
number of conference rooms	1
typical workspace	72 sf

Photography Credits:
Assassi
Copyright 2002

4

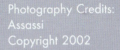

5

6

7 Loft Bedroom
8 First Floor Plan
9 Second Floor Plan
10 Exploded Axonometric
11 Conference Room

7

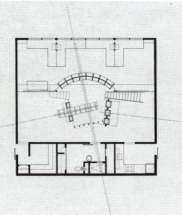

8

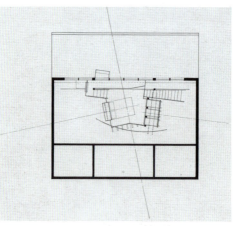

9

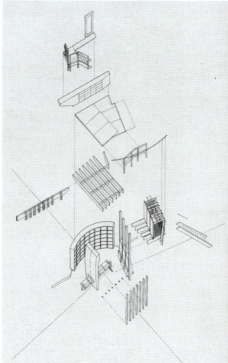

10

Bullock, Smith & Partners, Inc.

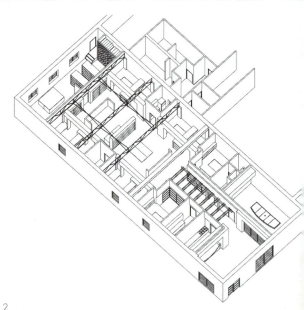

1

06

Bullock, Smith & Partners, Inc. has offices located in Knoxville and Nashville, Tennessee. The Nashville program called for offices and work area for approximately twelve to fourteen architects and staff, conference room and lobby, and support spaces. An existing one-story warehouse, previously used for light industry in an area of town known for its adaptive reuse projects, was purchased for their firm.

The architect conceived of the space as an office-as-village. This was achieved by creating circulation paths (streets and plazas) in plan and visually separating the geometric masses (buildings) from the sky (ceiling) in section. Bold colors were used to delineate function and orientation; red was used at 'exterior' perimeter walls, yellow for the 'main street' and 'plaza' edge, white for walls both floating and punctured, blue for accent and service spaces, and gray for the 'sky'. Existing structural elements were celebrated as found conditions.

Through the process of layering planes and colors, vistas are created within the dynamic and playful workspace.

2

date of completion	1998
number of employees	9
total square footage	4,785
number of conference rooms	2
typical workspace size	100 sf

1 Reception Desk
2 Plan Axonometric
3 Firm Graphics Drawings
4 Office
5 Graphic Display
6 Studio
7 Lobby
8 Central Corridor

Photography Credits:
Bill LaFevor

3

4

5

7

8

6

Dasic Architects

1

Dasic Architects is an architecture firm located in Tokyo, Japan. In Tokyo it is very common to convert apartments to and from offices. The spaces are often designed to serve both purposes, depending on tenant.

The firm's office is a two level apartment inside with an exposed clad concrete facade. The first and second level are connected through a 'double space galleria' above the kitchen space. The upper floor has a spiral staircase, leading to a roof deck which gives a spectacular view of Shinjuku skyscrapers.

The goal was to create a studio with lots of natural light, where the architects could work with an assistant during the day and receive clients as well. The glass walls and the ceiling glass create an atmosphere of space bathed in natural sunlight.

The materials are simple white paint with wood floors, giving the space a sense of a modern apartment and a modern office – comfortable but businesslike. The walls contain framed graphic art, generally by European artists. The furniture is based on a German modular Haller system. Although it is a standard prefabricated system, all of the elements and pieces are custom designed and assembled. The modular system allows for various configurations as needs within the firm change.

07

2

3

date of completion	1987
number of employees	8
total square footage	1,300
number of conference rooms	2
typical workspace size	70 sf

Photography Credit:
Peter M. Cook
CAD model:
Dasic Architects

5

4

6

7

Elliott + Associates

2

08

administrative staff, as well as showcasing a gallery/conference space to accommodate project meetings, small social gatherings, the display of project photographs and the exhibition of one changing artwork. The second floor level houses the studio, where workstations are located on the north side to benefit from the soft light, while the lunch room/library is placed on the south in the south sunlight. A large central work counter/ material library allows open access to all professionals.

The architectural concept for the Heierding Building interior focused on 'Light Shrines.' The firm concentrated on using the daylight coming into the space to create the atmosphere. There are a total of six shrines in the building that illustrate how light can behave as it interacts with the architecture. The goal was to use light as a design element and "paint with light." Light is the art and the spirit of the space.

Light Shrine 1 — A bare bulb hanging from the ceiling at the "nose" of the building that emits "energy" of the building. It remains on 24 hours a day.

Light Shrine 2 — The triangular reception space formed by theater scrim "holding" the shadows from exterior windows and "capturing" the light inside.

Light Shrine 3 — Lighted "slit" panel in the men's toilet and visible through the clerestory glass.

Elliott+Associates Architects is an architecture firm located in Oklahoma City, Oklahoma. In 1995 the firm chose to move the office back downtown as an expression of both architectural preservation and modern thinking. This decision was made through various brainstorming sessions conducted with the staff to define project scope and needs. The selected restoration and renovation project was the Heierding Building, which is listed on the National Register of Historic Places. Elliott+Associates focused on returning the exterior to its 1914 condition and to meet the required ADA requirements without compromising the integrity of the historic structure.

The site concept included restoring the immediate site and sidewalks, as well as creating "a patch of green" on the adjacent property, in direct contrast to the hardscape of the downtown setting.

The two level office includes an administrative level on the first floor and the studio on level two. The first floor program facilitates the

1

date of completion	1995
number of employees	15
total square footage	5,080
number of conference rooms	1
typical workspace size	96 sf

Photography Credits:
Robert Shimer

5

3

Light Shrine 4 — Lighted stair risers allowing you to "walk on light."

Light Shrine 5 — Back lighted roof drain pipe that illuminates the acute angle corner of the interior brick.

Light Shrine 6 — Solar mesh "light walls" dividing the studio work stations.

In addition to focal light concepts, Elliott+Associates used a variety of common materials in unusual and thought provoking ways. Twelve foot long pull chain switches were used in lieu of wall switches. Theatrical scrim is used as space dividers instead of glass to create visual privacy between spaces. Perforated hardboard ceilings with batt insulation above act as a good acoustical surface. Clear fiberglass pipe normally used for solar water storage tubes are incorporated as ductwork to communicate that air is invisible and "light." High tech nylon fabric is used as air supply ducts in the studio. It "breathes" as supply air is discharged into the space. Fiberglass mesh solar shades are used on the interior to form "light walls" at the workstations, to soften the light and create a better ambiance for computer use.

4

6

7

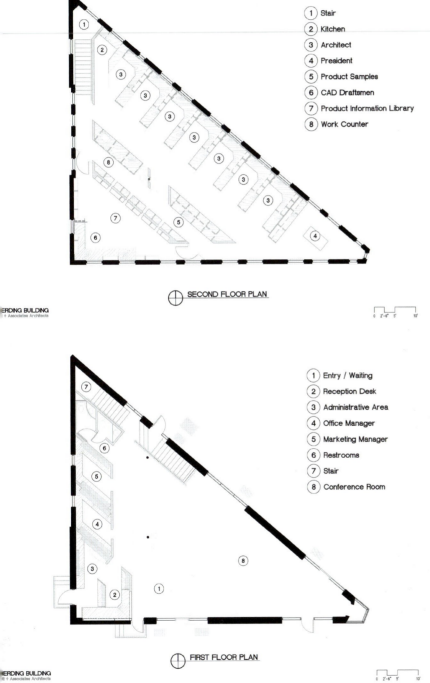

1	Stair
2	Kitchen
3	Architect
4	President
5	Product Samples
6	CAD Draftsmen
7	Product Information Library
8	Work Counter

⊕ SECOND FLOOR PLAN

ERDING BUILDING
+ Associates Architects

0 2'-6" 5'   10'

10

1	Entry / Waiting
2	Reception Desk
3	Administrative Area
4	Office Manager
5	Marketing Manager
6	Restrooms
7	Stair
8	Conference Room

⊕ FIRST FLOOR PLAN

ERDING BUILDING
+ Associates Architects

0 2'-6" 5'   10'

Gentile Holloway O'Mahoney

1

2

09

Gentile Holloway O'Mahoney & Associates, Inc. is a landscape architecture, planning, and environmental consulting firm, originally established in 1988. The firm has remained at ten or under in number of employees for its history, operating as one studio size.

In 1998 a separate group was formed to buy land and build an office building. The partners, an architect, a general contractor and a landscape architect, created a skillful group, with each utilizing their expertise to end with a cost effective and unique project. The firms of these partners now together lease the finished building.

The previous office had been confined to a shot-gun setup with very limited space. A typical situation that many designers find themselves in – a major client was across the hall. But the firm was outgrowing its space and was ready for a move. The entry courtyard became a functional asset to the business as it is used as a classroom from the conference room. Clients request to come and use the conference room for items peripheral to the firm's involvement in the project.

Design studios operate differently among professions. This firm has attempted to address this in the layout. The office operates as one large space. The only two doors provide privacy for the conference room and the partner's office. Each employee benefits by seeing each of the firm's projects progress through the office, through drawings, specifications, telephone conversations, meetings, etc.

The three partners' offices anchor the building in each corner. In the center of the open floor plan are two ten foot 'blitz' tables set at counter height, used for organizing, collating, charrettes, and rendering. The unique bookshelf/dividers are used between the partners' offices and the general work area. These units house personal reference material, samples, and display items.

Due to the nature of the work with large drawings, the firm designed large layout spaces at each workstation. There are four general workstations, with computers located in the corners. These four stations can be expanded to eight as the need arises. Roll files were also designed at each desk.

date of completion	2000
number of employees	10
total square footage	2400
number of conference rooms	1
typical workspace size	50–90sf

4

1 Studio
2 Typical Workstation
3 Printing/Filing Area
4 Courtyard
5 Exterior
6 1907 Lobby Entrance

Photography Credits:
Emily O'Mahoney 3
Kevin Smith 1, 2, 4, 5, 6

5

3

6

Joyce Signs

10

Joyce Signs is a young architectural signage company with new offices designed by archimania™. The firm is located within a turn-of-the-century retail building in an historic urban district. Currently undergoing revitalization, the historic district is attracting artists, galleries and diverse creative professionals.

The goal was to design an office space that was cost effective and reflected the company's vibrant and creative approach to serving its clients. The project consists of a conference room, work stations for designers, sales offices and production areas.

One of the main design considerations was maintaining openness between functions in order to facilitate communication, while simultaneously creating privacy for each distinct function. This was achieved by the use of transparent acrylic panels that defined space, while allowing light to pass through, visually opening up the space. Standard 4x8 sheets of plywood turned on end were used to create partial walls around the sales office, giving greater privacy.

The use of color, simple materials and the utilization of existing walls and infrastructure where possible solved budgetary constraints. Color breaks up the spaces and provides visual layers as each space progresses away from the glass front.

date of completion	2002
number of employees	6
total square footage	1550
number of conference rooms	2
typical workspace size	64 sf

1 Main Corridor
2 Tiled Wall w/ Acrylic Panels
3 Layering of Color and Materials
4 Conference Room
5 Workstations

Photography Credits:
Jeffrey Jacobs/Arch. Photo. Inc.

4

3   5

Odle & Young Architects

1

Odle & Young Architects, Inc. is located in downtown Knoxville, Tennessee. The firm took an old building with character on the edge of, and a part of, a Historical Neighborhood and restored the building by maintaining its solid character and adding modern features.

11

The 2-story historical building was originally known as the 'Rogers Building' and later as the 'Wylie Hardware Building' (circa 1904). The open plan studio is located on the lower level with leasable space on the second floor.

The entry is located at the rear of the building, adjacent to parking, in lieu of being located on the five-lane highway to the front of the building. The original brick facade is modernized with a glass and steel, transparent, triangular structure entry element. Upon entry, the visitor is greeted by three arched brick portals and a lobby which accesses the shared formal conference room, accessible toilets and the vertical circulation element.

The stair extends through the $2\frac{1}{2}$ story light well which brings light into the center of the lobby. The architect's studio is visible through the tall glass walls of the lightwell and is accessed through the relocated, original door and transom.

2

date of completion	2002
number of employees	7
total square footage	1,350
number of conference rooms	1
typical workspace (average)	56 sf

1 Front Facade
2 Stairway
3 Circular Studio Windows
4 Main Entry Nightscape
5 Formal Conference Room
6 Archways at Lobby

Photography Credits:
Steve Young

The open studio plan includes five foot high panel dividers for each workstation, an eight feet x four feet informal meeting/work table, the product library featuring a rolling ladder system and two larger workstations for the two principals located in each of the storefront windows.

This innovative project was a finalist for the Metropolitan Planning Commission's Excellence Award and received recognition from Knox Heritage for commercial restoration.

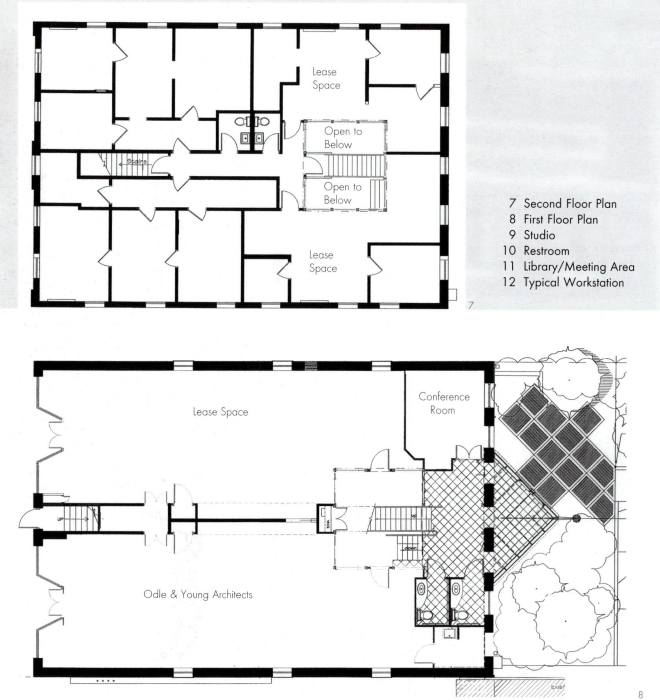

7 Second Floor Plan
8 First Floor Plan
9 Studio
10 Restroom
11 Library/Meeting Area
12 Typical Workstation

Lease Space

Open to Below

Open to Below

Stairs

Lease Space

Lease Space

Conference Room

Odle & Young Architects

Serrao Design/Architecture

1

2

12

Serrao Design/Architecture is a small firm located in San Francisco, California. The South of Market loft space allows for maximum efficiency, as well as maximum flexibility for the current staff of four. A customized system of shelving and workstations were developed and positioned along one sidewall of the space. This system, acting as a formal and spatial armature, is both a point of reference and spatial organizer, as well as the primary container of all records and material for the studio. Allowing for flexibility and transformability, all workstations, tables and storage units are customized to standard repetitive modules and set on casters. With this, the space can transform and be reorganized as the needs of the studio and the work changes. These transformations can occur with ease on a daily basis. The armature, as well as the workstations, translucent partitions and furniture, work together to form a common kit of parts made up of simple steel fabrications that bolt together for ease of assembly. Supporting the industrial language of many of the elements and the notion of loft space, all light fixtures are customized using standard electrical components.

3

date of completion	2000
number of employees	4
total square footage	1,100
number of conference rooms	1
typical workspace	85 sf

Photography Credits:
Frederic Neema

4 7

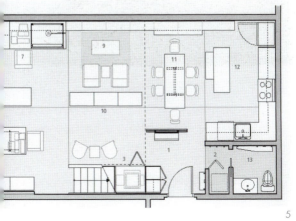

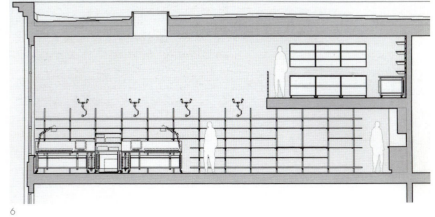

5 6

Spiral Co., Ltd.

architectural
photography

graphic design

art

13

1

2

3

Spiral Co., Ltd. Is a unique atelier located in Mitaka, Tokyo. It would be very easy for visitors to miss the building, as the frontage of the atelier is only two meters. A large wooden door invites one into the atelier through a side porch lined with tall dry walls, but with no ceiling, giving the feeling of an outside porch. The gallery follows the porch, where the light comes through the windows at foot level.

Taking off one's shoes at the end of the gallery, the visitor descends several steps to enter the studio. Koji Kobayashi, a well-known architectural photographer in Japan, is the owner of this atelier. He also acts as an Art Director, who curates exhibitions of ''Modern Japanese'' using silk, porcelains, Okinawa Glass works, etc. His creations include screens, rolls, lamps and many other items, using his own photos and these traditional Japanese materials.

date of completion	1994
number of employees	4
total square meters	129
number of conference rooms	1
typical workspace (average)	varies

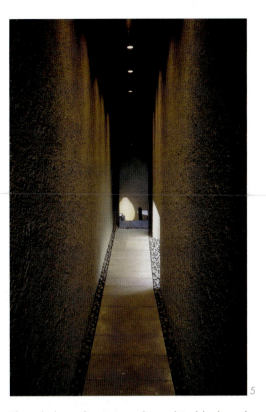

1 Entry
2 Gallery w/ Low Window Wall
3 Stairway
4 Exterior from Inner Court
5 Porch followed by the Gallery
6 Nightview of the Gallery

His interests focus on "fusion." Though it often utilizes traditional materials, it is not "retrospective" or "conservative" at all, but modern and sophisticated. So his atelier, with architect Michimasa Kawaguchi, is worked out to a very "modern and traditional" Japanese building.

The whole atelier is coordinated in black and white. However, the materials that compose these colors are very natural and traditional things. For instance, all the wooden parts had been painted in "Sumi," or Japanese ink, and hundreds of kneaded Japanese Papers have been applied to the wall and the ceiling.

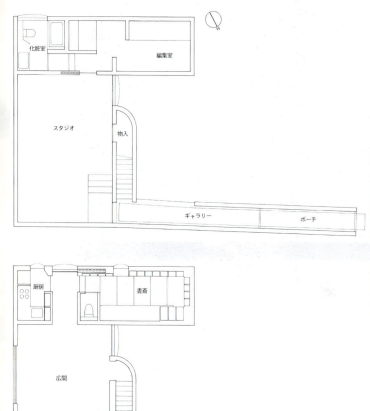

7

9

10

8

11

12

13

14

15

Watson Tate Savory

architecture

1

2

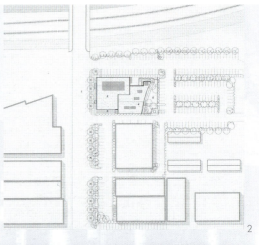

3

14

The office of Watson Tate Savory is an adaptive reuse of an existing one-story, light industrial warehouse, which had been in partial use as a storage shed and partially abandoned. The building was renovated as a speculative venture for tenant fit-up. The rear portion of the building comprises the architects' office.

As a project designed by a client group for its own use, the office of Watson Tate Savory provides not only a chance to explore a vanishing urban industrial fabric, but also an opportunity to express to a growing community the possibilities inherent in older, historically unremarkable buildings.

Programmatic requirements for Watson Tate Savory include work stations with expansion space for a staff of twenty, a conference room, a reference library, a kitchenette, a reception area and storage. Spaces are organized around a matrix of public/private functions in response to an L-shaped shell. The interior is modulated by a series of horizontal and vertical planes bisecting a central administration and research pavilion. Wood panels, arranged in sequence, fracture and further articulate the space, which is composed through a system of geometric overlays of squares and golden sections. Light is introduced, not only through existing window openings, but also through newly constructed clerestory "monitors", built over existing openings that once contained industrial skylights.

Situated alongside a railroad cut used for the transport of industrial freight, the north facade of the office curves in response to a fragment of a rail delivery spur that originally tied to the

date of completion	1990
number of employees	10
total square footage	4,520
number of conference rooms	1.5
typical workspace (average)	55

Photography Credits:
G.MatsonPhoto

5

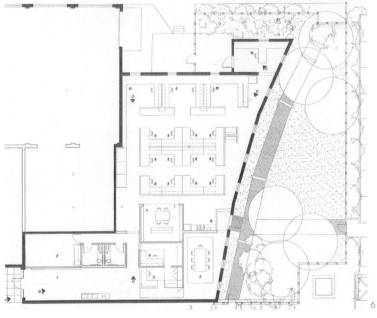

6

4

main track. Surrounding the site, other fragments of an earlier industrial age dependent on the railroad remain as well, in various stages of prosperity and decay.

As this immediate neighborhood is revitalized and developed into a new commercial district, it is these fragments of a modest bygone industrial community that this project seeks to engage. By utilizing simple industrial materials found in the immediate neighborhood and by intervening delicately in the existing structure, the design attempts to provide a point of repose from which to consider the contribution of background buildings to the patina of a particular urban experience.

Wexler/Kollman

15

Soaring space mixed with natural lighting were the main objectives when architects Stuart Wexler and Michael Kollman began renovating the old Hershberger Community Center in Prairie View, Illinois, a northern suburb of Chicago. Built in 1895, the two-story wood-framed structure had most recently been home to American Legion Post 1247 and featured an impressive beaded fir arched ceiling and walls, complimented by a vintage fir floor. Those unique aspects were returned to their original luster when the office of Wexler/Kollman P.C., Ltd. moved into the top floor in 1990.

When originally constructed, the building was placed atop limestone block piers and remained open under the first floor. To increase energy efficiency and discourage inhabitation of animals and debris, the building was raised about three feet. This allowed for the design of an English basement with natural light.

date of completion	1990
number of employees	4
total square footage	1900
number of conference rooms	2
typical workspace	200 sf

1 Community Center ca. 1895
2 Exterior Prior to Renovation
3 Exterior
4 Gallery
5 Exterior/Signage
6 Conference Area

Photography Credits:
Michael S. Kollman

5

6

The existing one-story concrete block kitchen was replaced with an entry stair tower to improve circulation. The three-story tower includes a unique loft conference room for the architects, reached by iron spiral stairs and tops-off their creative office space.

The architectural studio space is punctuated with light and soaring volume. It features offices, storage and conference space in a unique setting. The vast openness is divided down the middle with a built-in bookcase unit, providing separation between the gallery and private offices. Walls extend to eight feet high with clear glass transoms above. The original fir floor defines the open studio space.

In keeping with the historical significance of the site, the land has been restored to its native prairie origins. Native wildflowers and prairie grasses, along with burr oaks, have been reintroduced and are adapting well.

The $150,000 renovation project provided about 1,900 square feet for the four-person firm. The project exceeds each of the criteria set at the beginning – affordability, adaptability to needs, suitability for leasing, and the uniqueness and creativity of the space.

Architecture Project

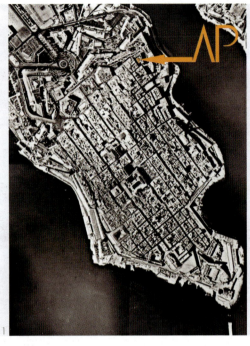

The seventeenth century fabric of the building was considerably tampered with during the nineteenth century and during the Crimean War, when Malta served as headquarters for the allies, an unrealized project for a military hospital on the bastion incorporated this building to serve as the entrance wing. In spite of these changes, the building is the only one to retain its original aspect, most of the area having been redeveloped in the nineteenth century in the eclectic style of the period.

16

Architecture Project was set up in May 1991 to provide a complete range of architectural services, with special focus on restoration and design. Over the years an international team of architects and researchers has grown to form the main core of staff, committed to evolving the main interests of the firm. These include a concern with context, both physical and cultural, and the reciprocal relationship between the built work and the environment; research in energy efficiency in order to minimize the building's dependence on non-renewable resources; and the rehabilitation and revitalization of historic buildings.

The building which houses the offices of Architecture Project is situated on the landward bastions of the sixteenth century fortified town of Valletta, and overlooks the entrance to Marsamxett Harbour. A tunnel underlying the building and running along its length connects the street to the fortified ditch below and forms part of the original defense system.

date of completion	1996
number of employees	29
total square meters	393
number of conference rooms	2
typical workspace	8 sqm

The layout is centered around the main open plan working space on the second floor which, together with a mezzanine level introduced in the high 'piano nobile' when the offices moved to the new premises, accommodates approximately twenty five work stations. The mezzanine floor consists of a steel and wood deck that spans the length of the space and is suspended from the beams of the roof. This main working area also incorporates the reception and the principal conference room, the latter participating visually with the activity of the office, while providing the necessary privacy when the need arises.

Several rooms at intermediate levels provide quiet areas, or allow the more messy and noisy activities, such as model making, to be segregated from the main work areas. They are grouped around the ground floor courtyards that belong historically to the first phase of the building of Valletta and have a separate entrance on Sappers Lane. The two offices at first floor, on the other hand, are used to absorb the fluctuating needs of the office and house the workstations of temporary staff and researchers or the numerous students who join the office as part of their training.

5 Ground Floor Plan
6 First Floor Plan
7 Second Floor Plan
8 Mezzanine Plan
9 Conference Room
10 Stairway
11 Library
12 Mezzanine
13 Studio

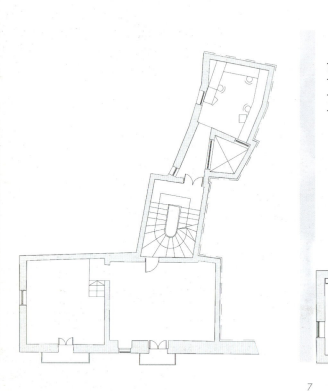

6

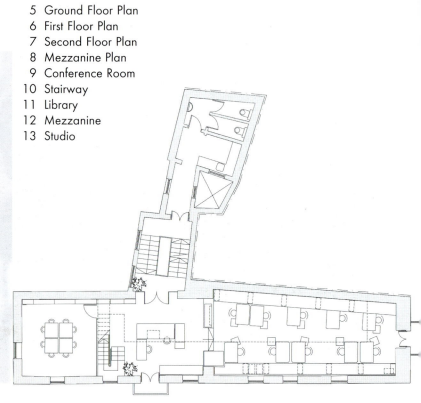

7

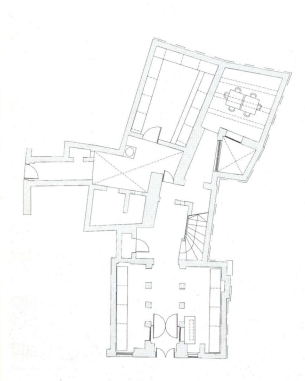

5

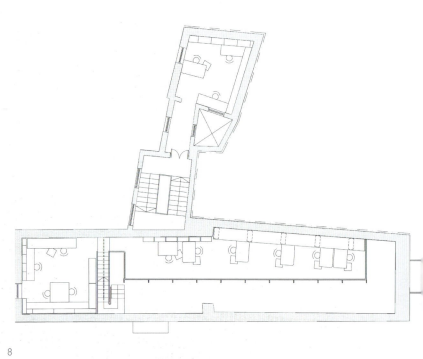

8

9

10

11

12

13

Ashton Raggatt McDougall

architecture
urban design
masterplanning

1

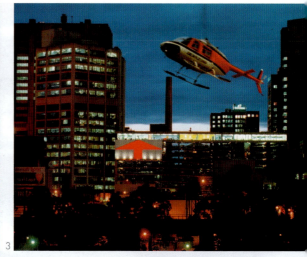

3

2

17

Ashton Raggatt McDougall, or ARM, is a cutting edge design consultancy, regarded as Australia's leader in computer generated design, computer imaging and presentation of the "virtual" building. The firm's design studio is located on one level on top of a ten storey carpark. The office has a continuous wall of glass on the south side, providing terrific views to the Yarra River, with the railway viaduct in front and the casino beyond, the shrine of remembrance to the east and Port Phillip Bay on the horizon to the west. The principal concept for the office layout was to keep this view "public" by making a wide, polished-concrete walkway along the glass, with working spaces opening directly from it. Large sliding doors provide occasional separation but most of the time it functions as the primary office circulation.

The reception area includes an award wall which contains forty state, national, and international awards. Selected models, easel panels, books and magazines are also displayed in the gracious waiting area.

date of completion	1997
number of employees	30
total square meters	780
number of conference rooms	2
typical workspace size	8 sqm

Photography Credit:
Ashton Raggatt McDougall
John Gollings 1, 3, 4, 5, 6

4

5

The three principals of ARM spend much of their time in the design Studio, but also share a space open to the main window wall circulation spine. This 'home base' provides the opportunity for ad hoc conversations and perhaps uninterrupted time. Associates do not have separate offices but work directly with their project team in the open plan studio. The product material library lines the walls of the staff room. Adjoining the lunch room is the image library, where all hard copy presentation material, submission, slides, video, etc. are stored and catalogued. The lunch room is in the middle of the long linear office and makes the link between the front of house areas of reception, administration, meeting rooms, archive and image library and the design studio, model making, print and server areas.

6

Babey Moulton Jue & Booth

1

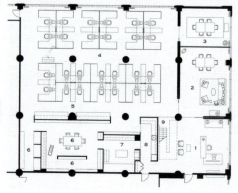

3

18

Babey Moulton Jue & Booth is an interior design firm with an international reputation, founded in 1991 by principals Pamela Babey, David Moulton, Gerald Jue and Michael Booth. The firm is located in an area called SOMA (south of Market) in San Francisco, which has progressively become a popular area for renovation.

After a time of tight quarters as the firm grew quickly, a 9,000 sf industrial building was chosen for renovation. The structure included a variety of unique spaces that the interior design firm could easily see potential. As in many industrial buildings where there are minimal windows; this structure brought a treasure to the firm as they uncovered a full window wall under layers of stucco. These windows opened onto a two-story space with an adjacent mezzanine.

This large volume of space and wonderful quality of light was the perfect location for the open studio. Also located on the first floor are the entry, reception, conference rooms and library. Partners' offices occupy the mezzanine level and mimic desks as larger versions of the studio desks below.

The passion of the firm is illustrated with the use of furnishings, color, artwork and project examples. A collage of furniture gives character to each space — each piece having a meaning and story as they are displayed on a pallette of white walls, ceiling, and ductwork. The floors are a combination of rich red tones, polished white floors, with accent rugs and base tones of tan.

For every client who enters the firm, the red carpet is rolled out. Attention to detail and meticulous selection of materials are illustrated with product samples throughout the office, which become living works of art for all projects. The firm's projects are diverse, including hospitality, residential, senior care, commercial office, banking, retail and public facilities. The firm is currently undergoing an expansion to 15,000 sf.

2

date of completion	1997
number of employees	35
total square footage	9000
number of conference rooms	2
typical workspace size	80 sf

Photography Credits:
Mark Darley Interior &
Architectural PhotographyEsto
Photographic

6

4

5

7

The Berger Partnership, P.S.

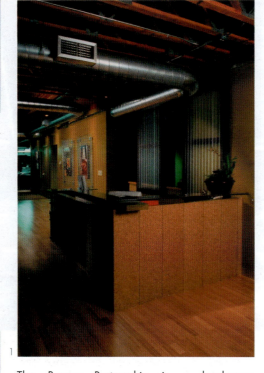

19

The Berger Partnership is a landscape architecture and site planning firm located in Seattle, Washington. The firm has occupied the same office since its inception, thirty years ago. As the result of continued growth, a move to a larger office was required. The design concept for the new office began by distributing a survey to the staff. Common feedback communicated an interest in maintaining the casual "boathouse" feeling of the old office, which included exposed wood and brick walls, open truss ceilings and an open floor plan. Sustainable and recyclable materials were requested, as well as a playful reflection of landscape architectural elements.

The new office, completed in April of 2001, includes small items which are reminiscent of the previous office space. The reception desk, for example, is made of recycled seed board and features a cornflower blue base (the color of the old office) with a portion of the original wrought iron fence.

As requested, many familiar aspects of the old building were duplicated in the design of the new space. An open lightwell and wide staircase were constructed between two formerly unattached floors. In addition to being a main circulation route between floors, the stairs are an amphitheater for Monday morning office meetings. Exposed ceiling structure and ducts have been duplicated from the former office, as well as an emphasis on the view of Lake Union. A canoe was purchased for use at lunch in the previous office and now holds a prominent location in the new office.

Color choices of eggplant, deep burgundy, cornflower blue and various shades of green portray a casual and creative environment. Recycled and sustainable materials are apparent through the office, such as bamboo hardwood floors, recycled fiber carpet and seed board casework.

The use of galvanized metal for trim and accent recalls outdoor metal finishes. Corrugated fiberglass panels recall a gardener's greenhouse or potting shed.

The Berger Partnership successfully attained an open and creative working environment through the use of materials and textures, the creation of volume and the accentuation of views.

date of completion	2001
number of employees	38
total square footage	6,000
number of conference rooms	2
typical workspace size	64 sf
manufactured workstations	yes

1 Reception Desk
2 Floor Plans
3 Display Wall w/ Steel Mesh Panels
4 Concrete Feature Wall

Photography Credits:
Richard Nicol

Workstations by:
Wattson Office Furniture of
Bainbridge Island, Washington

3

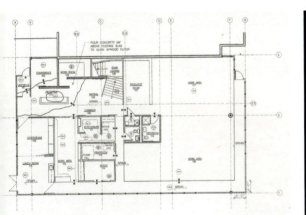

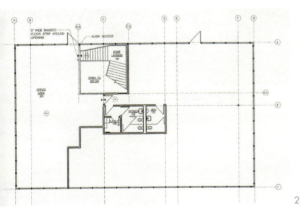

2

4

5   Kitchen
6   Stair
7   Canoe at Balcony
8   Studio
9   Workstation
10 Conference Room

Bullock, Smith & Partners, Inc.

architecture

landscape
architecture

20

The Knoxville, Tennessee offices of Bullock, Smith & Partners, Inc. are located in what was once the city's Southern Railway Station. Shortly after the firm was founded, it played a critical role in the design and renovation of the station.

The Southern Railway Station of Knoxville was built in 1903-1904, and was designed by the architect for the Southern Railway Company, Frank P. Milburn. Originally, the lower level of the Southern Railway Station contained the mail, express, telegraph, and dining rooms for the baggage area. Designed in the "Jim Crow" era, the upper level consisted of segregated waiting rooms which both opened to the ticket office. These waiting areas each contained a smoking room, ladies' parlor and restrooms. The adjacent freight depot was originally symmetrical and linked to the main building with a breezeway. In 1945 the station was 'modernized' and the central clock tower and chimneys were removed. This time period may have been the time in which the glass blocks were added throughout the space.

The Freight Depot or Railway Express building, also built in 1903-1904, was expanded in 1911. The original building, also designed by Frank P. Milburn, was the one-story section to the east. Eleven years later, the two and one-half story pavilion (which now houses the main entrances and reception area for the interior design firm Corporate Interiors) and the one-story west flank were added. They were separated by fourteen feet of covered breezeway from the original building.

Interesting architectural features of the Southern Railway Station include fireplaces featuring inscriptions by Robert Burns, the Scottish poet, and coffered ceilings in the former two passenger waiting rooms and the former restaurant on the ground level. New paint colors matching the original brick and stone have been used, as well as the composition roof that creates an illusion matching the original slate roof. Both buildings exhibit Neoclassical Revival with Jacobean/Dutch Colonial influence on the exterior, featuring corbel-stepped gables and windows of a neo-classical palladia motif. The construction is a combination of brick, wood, and cast iron.

Passenger service stopped in 1970. The building was vacant and suffered a variety of water and fire damage, until purchased at auction by the Southern Station Partnership in 1988. Renovation of the property took place in 1989, in conjunction with the Knoxville Streetscape project on Depot Avenue. The original L-shaped staircases were straightened and demising walls added to permit separate tenants.

date of completion	1989
number of employees	23
total square footage	10,400
number of conference rooms	3
typical workspace size	64 sf

Photography Credits:
David Luttrell 1, 2, 7
Bullock, Smith & Partners 4, 5, 6, 8

In deciding how to deploy the various spaces needed for the firm throughout the upper levels of the renovated railway station, the designers took their cues from the nature of an architecture firm and from the nature and hierarchy of spaces in the building itself. The building is elongated and symmetrical about the main two-story lobby. It is divided into two primary spaces, formerly the waiting rooms, and other secondary and service spaces.

Two primary spaces are designed as open office plans with centrally located, group-oriented and circulation spaces. Some such spaces in the west wing are the awards and display corridor, the small conference room, the design review corridor and the planning room — a room with a large table where charettes and other drawing-intensive work sessions take place. Along the perimeter of each former waiting room are located the individual workspaces, benefitting from direct access to light, but maintaining a continuous band of circulation along the exterior wall. The secondary and service zones contain the kitchen and lounge, model-making and presentation staging areas, storage spaces, and restrooms.

Although there was no evidence of much of an original color scheme, the new interior and exterior colors were based in a general way on color preferences of the era. The brick used throughout the station is beige, as seen on the fireplaces; however, it had been painted on the exterior and the removal of the paint would have been costly and time-consuming. Therefore, new paint colors matching the brick and stone were used.

Canizaro Cawthon Davis

1

21

modern workplace. Two buildings were renovated into 21,000 sq. ft. of office space, while four badly deteriorated buildings were demolished. Everywhere possible, the existing building was left intact and untouched — preserving the past and providing opportunities for education in both construction techniques and the history of the building.

The Architect's Statement became to 'seize serendipity, embrace disharmony, and trust the design build process. Make decisions, make them quickly, and know we cannot make them all. Realize the limit of our reach. Make the right decisions, those that set design in motion, and let others follow.'

Canizaro Cawthon Davis is an architecture, planning, and interior design firm located in downtown Jackson, Mississippi. The Owner/ Architect purchased the 1907 S.N. Thomas' Sons Building in February 2000, with the desire to renovate and re-use the existing complex to create a pleasing and efficient office space for a mid-size architecture firm, leasable tenant space, and on-site parking. Goals included wanting to highlight the merchant history of the building while contrasting it with new construction, benefit the City by maintaining its past, and complete the project, from purchase to move-in, in five months.

Though the building was never intended to provide for the functions it does today, Canizaro Cawthon Davis simply adapted the building to their needs. Although the firm's needs are very specific, the building is not so tuned to those needs that it can easily become obsolete. The ''loose fit'' is what gives the building a new life. The building and the firm's energy can also be seen through various 'blind art' designs on the front facade of the building. An architect can bring much life to a building — a constant design in progress — even through the simplicity of designs illustrated through blinds, of which the city of Jackson enjoyed over the year following completion of the renovation.

The Architect worked closely with The Department of Archives and History and the City of Jackson to save the traditional character of the building, while creating a

2

3

date of completion	2000
number of employees	21
total square footage	9,500
number of conference rooms	4
typical workspace size	100 sf

1 Exterior After
2 'Blind Art'
3 Exterior Before
4 Lobby and Stair
5 Screen at Reception
6 Marqee Signage

Photography Credits:
Canizaro Cawthon Davis
Tom Joynt Photography –
Images 4, 7, 9, 10

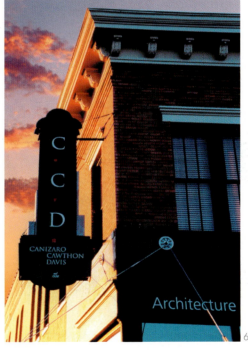

CIVITAS

landscape
architecture
urban designers
planners

1

22

Civitas, Inc. is a landscape architecture and urban planning firm located in Denver, Colorado. The firm's new offices, in the sixty year old mechanic's warehouse building on the south edge of town, were designed by Semple Brown Design, P.C.

The building is a single story structure divided into three bays by bowstring trusses, which are supported on steel pipe columns and enclosed with a masonry perimeter wall.

While the project primarily involved the interior of the building, the team approached the design as an urban planning project. The Civitas' employees are organized into five loose departments of design. The design team treated the whole office, in effect, as a city plan.

Through a variety of *urban studies*, an organization of the office components developed.

The design is organized about a main street and several side streets. Individual elements of the office program are integrated as *buildings*

within the shell of the warehouse. The main street extends through the space, anchored by the two most public spaces in the office, the new building entry and the Breakroom, which opens up to the alley and future site of the Denver Art Museum expansion. Employees ride their bicycles and scooters directly into the office through the glass garage door at this end of the *street*.

The southwest corner of the office is a small *storefront* conference room, which reveals itself to sidewalk passersby. During sunny afternoons, the fiberglass clad walls glow in the late-day sun, providing a buffer to the surrounding workstations.

The south edge of Main Street is defined with a variety of large scale elements: reception, conference, and workroom.

The north edge is defined with a series of workstation *neighborhoods*.

The design incorporates a relatively simple material palette, respectful of the simple warehouse building. The existing concrete floors have been stained and polished, the workstations are divided with MDF panels, and the reception counter is backed with clear maple panel and a cold-rolled steel shingle canopy.

date of completion	2001
number of employees	45
total square footage	15,000
number of conference rooms	4
typical workspace size	81 sf

1 Lobby
2 Typical Workstation
3 Lobby Rendering
4 Break Room

Photography Credits:
Ron Forth Photography

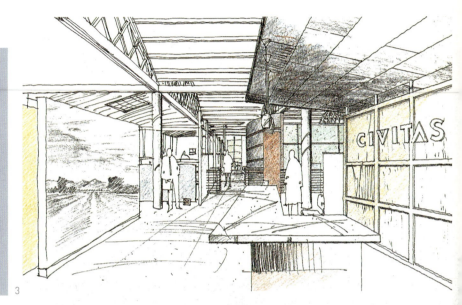

Civitas occupies 12,800 sf of the building and leases the remaining 2,200 sf. In the next two years, the firm plans to occupy this additional 2,200 sf and, in five years, the basement, which is an additional 1,900 sf, will be renovated. With simplicity and modularity of design, the workstation furniture and additional space should occur easily, as the entire building layout was masterplanned from the start.

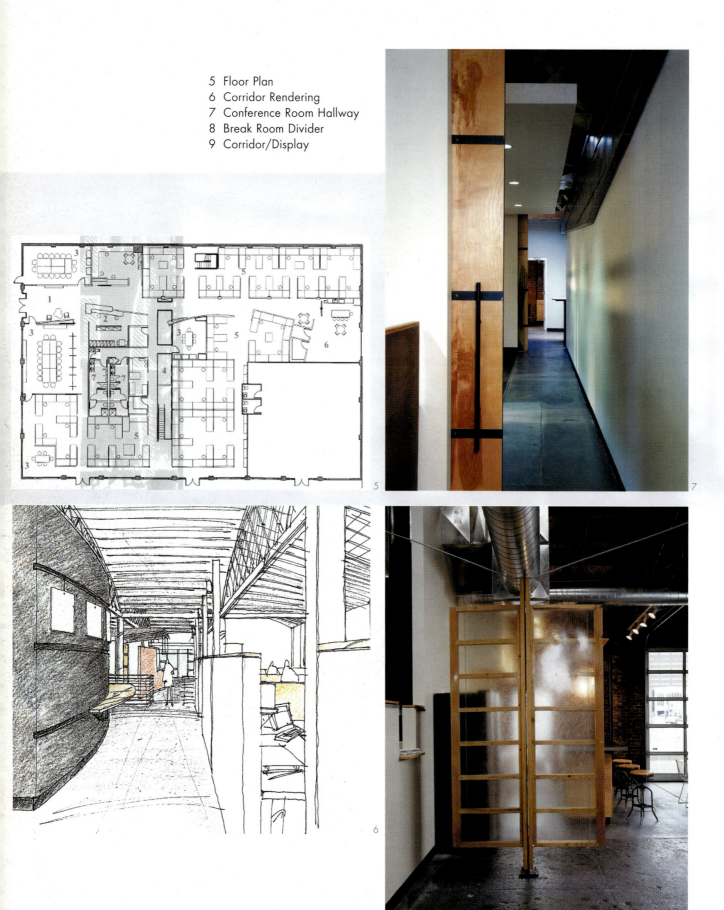

EDAW

landscape
architecture
environmental
urban planning

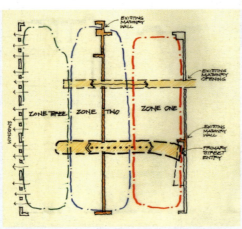

EDAW, Inc. is a landscape architecture, environmental, and urban planning firm located in Denver, Colorado. The architect for these new offices was Semple Brown Design, P.C.

23

The second floor warehouse space is contained in two adjacent buildings, which are connected through an existing masonry party wall. The space is organized into three landscapes: Urban, Mountain/Building, and Field/Ocean. The landscapes are tied together through the cross axis between the two building bays: a custom woven wood panel defining the primary spine.

The office entry incorporates the Urban Landscape. Hard surfaces and simple utilitatrian finishes define the street-like corridors and building edges.

The Mountain/Building Landscape is developed as rhythmic series of partitions, which abut the existing building masonry party wall. These represent the misty layers of mountain vista.

The Field/Ocean Landscape is used to an advantage on the most open exterior wall of the existing warehouse. From the carpet patterns to the workstation partitions, this landscape integrates the rhythmic waves of wheat fields and oceans throughout the design.

Simple materials are used throughout, keeping within the language of the utilitarian warehouse structure. Fiberglass panels in custom steel storefronts create a play of light and a range of privacy for the individual offices. Workstation partitions utilize conventional metal framing, which in themselves become a design element.

date of completion	2000
number of employees	40
total square footage	12,000
number of conference rooms	3
typical workspace size	80 sf

1 Ceiling Detail
2 Zoning Diagram
3 Entry
4 Studio
5 Diagram Urban Space
6 Diagram Mountain/Building
7 Diagram Field/Ocean

Photography Credits:
Ron Forth Photography

4

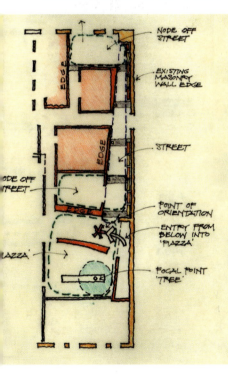

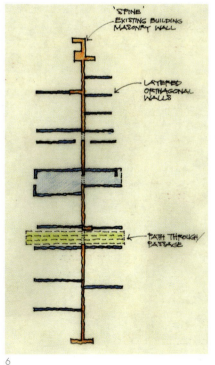

6

7

Steven Ehrlich Architects

architecture

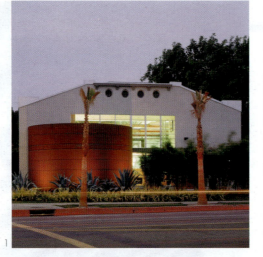

24

The soul of a derelict structure with a colorful history in Culver City, California was resurrected by Steven Ehrlich Architects. Built in 1917 as a dance hall and community center, the Culver City (Heart of Screenland) California Municipal Club House later found a second life as a mortuary. When the architects purchased the property for their offices it had been boarded up for years, a virtual "untouchable" stigmatized by its past.

A forensic visit to the building revealed several features that encouraged the purchase. Upon its conversion into a funeral parlor, the original structure's auditorium had been chopped into smaller spaces with hung ceilings; a semi-circular viewing room dominated the front of the building. Upon inspection a long-span wood truss roof system was found in the attic, and a maple floor where Culver City residents twirled between the wars was discovered beneath the old carpet.

The architects' challenge was to honor the spirit of the building (and its previous occupants) yet not to be a slave to its preservation, creating offices that would pulse with life and feature plenty of natural light and ventilation. While the post- "Alamo style" facade was judged to be of insufficient stature to warrant saving, budget constraints led to a decision not to alter principal roof lines and the building's footprint. The structure was stripped down to its essential shell.

A 90-year old rubber tree is the focal point of an outdoor courtyard, defined by a plastic "ornite" and wood-framed wall; a 14-ft square glass roll-up garage door dissolves the border between indoor and outdoor space and provides an abundance of natural light and air. A perimeter fixed wall of MDF with a clear finish defines the open work area. Aluminum provides a unifying accent on coffee and conference tabletops, bathroom counters, credenzas, and workstations. The workstations are made of Finland color birch plywood partitions and linoleum desktops on solid doors.

A model of inspired adaptive reuse, the office simultaneously embraces both the spiritual and environmental issues of recycling. On the material plane, the rejuvenation of a discarded structure conserves building materials and requires less energy to light, heat, and cool. At the same time, human dedication to a dynamic future converges with the past in the architects' conference room, formerly the mortuary's viewing room.

date of completion	1999
number of employees	30
total square footage	6,200
number of conference rooms	2
typical workspace	72 sf

1 Exterior
2 View from Courtyard into Office
3 Floor Plans
4 Stair

Photography Credits:
Marvin Rand

3   4

5 Exterior (New)
6 Exterior 1917
7 Entry
8 Studio

With a core and shell budget of $45/sf and a TI budget of $15 a foot, the offices' open plan reflects the "atelier" culture of this architectural practice. Longer spans required accommodating the openness of the library on the mezzanine and the ground-floor conference room led to the insertion of steel moment frames. Aluminum sash in a "thin line" detail inside and out evokes steel windows of the early twentieth century period.

Before the architects opened the doors of their new atelier, a sage-burning ceremony was conducted and holy water blessed by a local priest. All souls who might be lingering from days past were invited to attend.

5

6

7

Everton Oglesby Askew Architects

1

Established in 1991, Everton Oglesby Askew Architects is the fourth largest architectural firm in Nashville, Tennessee. With a passion for downtown, a concern for existing structures and a vision for the potential of the south of Broadway/Franklin Street area, in 1996, EOA bought and renovated the former St. Paul's African Methodist Episcopal Church, originally built in 1874. Following the congregation leaving downtown in the 1950's, the building has served several purposes, including being a warehouse facility until 1996.

25

The brutal post-church masonry wall along Fourth Avenue was removed to expose the original street front entries. New wood and glass doors and transoms were installed in the openings. Upon removal of the wall, round bricks and two column capitals were discovered in the rubble from the classically detailed portico. These findings are utilized as two short columns at the original bases. At the third portico base, a sculptural round brick column was designed to house the building entry and security kiosk as if growing out of a state of "ruins."

Through this reestablished street level entry, the visitor enters the buildings and "ascends" into the volume of the former sanctuary space through a wedged shaped slot, carved from the sanctuary floor. These entry stairs bring the visitor to a central gallery space that is used as a reception area and for display of the firm's work. The walls of the gallery angle toward a distant point to create a forced perspective toward the former "pulpit" area. Large acoustical screens atop the north gallery wall create a rhythm reinforcing the pulpit focus. New heavy timber fir posts and beams were added to the south side to enhance the rhythm as well.

The existing drywall ceiling at the bottom of the roof structure was removed to open the full volume of the sanctuary space to the Gallery and Design Studio. This exposed the original heavy timber roof structure and expanded the height of the space from 25' to 55'. The Franklin Street and Fourth Avenue windows, infilled over the years, were replaced to recall the fenestration of the original openings. The open studio space was placed on the north side of the sanctuary space to provide north light and a view of downtown. The "core" type functions, such as restrooms, resource areas, workroom and kitchen, were placed to the south side against the former windows to control light into the space. The sanctuary floor, hardwood oak floor scraps, installed over the course of years by members of the congregations, were refinished for the Gallery space.

2

date of completion	1996
number of employees	37
total square footage	13,010
number of conference rooms	5
typical workspace size	80

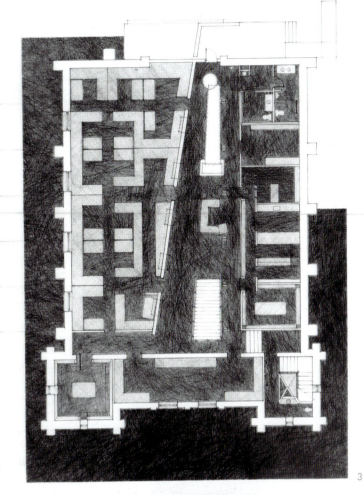

1 Exterior
2 Entry Stair
3 Floor Plan
4 Building Section

Photography Credits:
Tom Gatlin Photography

Graphics and Model
Photography Credits:
EOA Architects

3

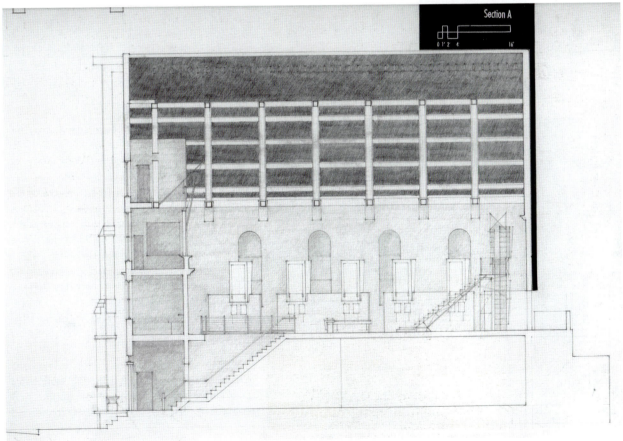

Section A

0 1' 2 4   16'

4

5

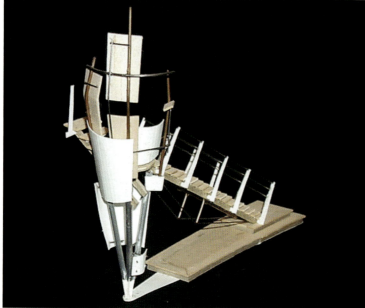

6

The infilled second floor of the northern tower was removed to form a tall two-story space, to serve as the firm's intimate conference room. The tackable walls at the perimeter provide the backdrop for the spaces' use as a "Crit Pit" for design creation, critique and presentation. The truncating walls above lean into the space and extend the height perception of the 24' tall space. The existing stair to the original choir loft balcony at the southern tower was maintained, for access to the larger capacity balcony Conference Room overlooking the volume of the sanctuary.

In 2000, the "mezzanine" was built-out as expansion space for additional staff. This natural expansion included the design and construction of the "pulpit" stair connecting the mezzanine to the studio level.

7

There are no desk cubicles or partitions in the office space, as the entire design staff works in the open studio space that was the former worship space. The design of the space promotes collaboration and learning as all levels of staff interact together. Intern Architects are encouraged to use the best resources available through the open studio plan, with accessible projects, resources, and staff.

8

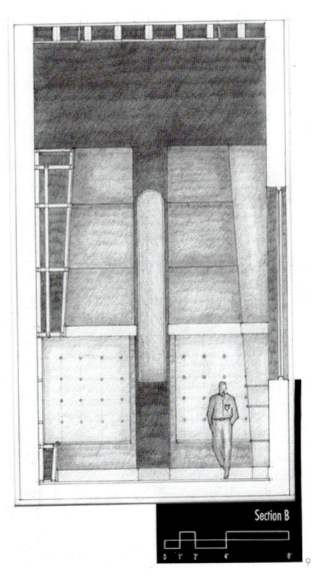

Section B

9

Frederick Fisher and Partners

architecture

1

Frederick Fisher and Partners is a leading Los Angeles architecture and planning firm, which owns the original 1950s-style offices of the late prominent architect A. Quincy Jones. Since 1995 Frederick Fisher and Partners has occupied the offices in West Los Angeles, and has renovated the distinctive space. The building was named a Historic-Cultural Landmark of Los Angeles in 2001.

26

Jones and his partner, Frederick Emmons, originally created their office design around the concept of melding indoor and outdoor environments. The building is wrapped around four distinct garden courtyards, with all but one room looking onto an outdoor space. Even this conference room has a skylight and indoor-planted garden of bamboo.

The building's 7,500 square-foot plan is marked by a meandering quality, in which each distinct room reveals itself from the one before. Each room features large windows, many of them floor to ceiling, which flood offices and the studio space with natural light. In the renovation, Fisher re-painted with the office's original colors, and has also included period furniture pieces throughout the building.

date of completion	1995
number of employees	25
total square footage	7,500
number of conference rooms	1
typical workspace	32 sf

1 Reception
2 Exterior
3 Studio
4 Lobby
5 Courtyard Garden
6 Principal's Office
7 Central Garden
8 Conference Room
9 Product Library

Photography Credits:
Tim Streetporter

Hans van Heeswijk Architects

architecture

27

The Dutch firm Hans van Heeswijk Architects was founded in 1985. Since that time the firm has worked on a large number of diverse projects, such as houses, office buildings, interior design and civil engineering works.

The design team is committed to the achievement of a high degree of consistency in the architecture of its projects. Clear compositions of volumes, logical floorplans and spacial architecture, through the integration of openess and light, form the main design aims. Moreover, the diverse designs show a high level of refinement and finishing in both detailing and material application.

In the millennium year 2000, the firm moved from the historical city centre to the East Harbour area of Amsterdam. These former harboursites have been recently rehabilitated and nowadays form a modern living and working area within walking distance of the historic city centre. The new self designed office building is situated beautifully in this water area with panoramic views.

The mixed-use building of Hans van Heeswijk Architects forms the head of a housing block. The building combines the designers' office on the waterfront side and an integrated gymnasium on the opposite side. The building and houses are separated by two all-glass set back stairhouses. The main entrance is situated prominently on the waterfront. The elevator leads visitors automatically to the reception desk at the topfloor. This floor, with conference tables next to the open corner windows, guarantees dynamic views up and across the former harbour. Obviously the main design theme is light and transparancy, contrasting the heavy brick and small windows of the neighbouring houses.

date of completion	2000
number of employees	24
total square meters	700
number of conference rooms	2
typical workspace (average)	8 sqm

Photography Credits:
Luuk Kramer
Amsterdam, The Netherlands

3

2

The four-story building consists of a slender regular construction of steel columns bearing thin concrete floors. This structure is wrapped in a wall of glass and wooden panels. All these components are precisely detailed, as exemplified by the use of open steel staircases, especially manufactured aluminum steps and self-designed furniture. Everything is designed in material application as industrial buildings.

With its transparent studios and the vertical stairhouse strips on either side, the building expresses the internal subdivision and structure most vividly at dark.

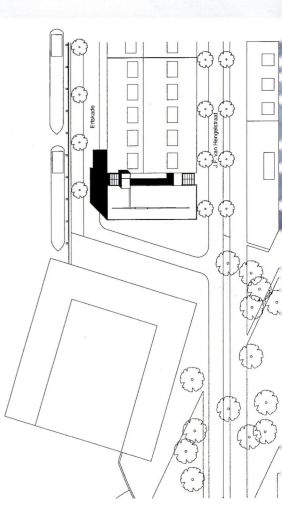

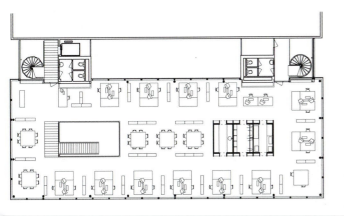

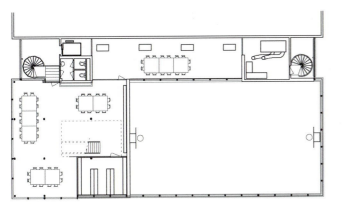

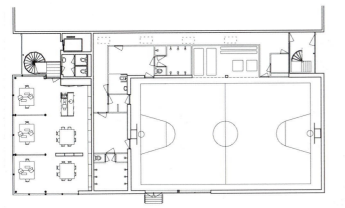

8

9

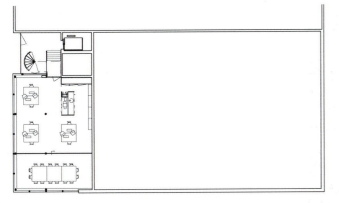

10

HMC Architects

architecture
planning
interior design

28

With office locations established throughout California and Nevada, including Ontario, Pasadena, San Diego, Sacramento, San Jose, Reno, and Las Vegas, HMC Architect's newest office in Irvine, California, presented design opportunities unique to its commercial office setting.

Situated in a multi-story office complex, HMC's design approach took full advantage of the first floor lobby location. The extensive use of uninterrupted floor-to-ceiling glass, combined with continual pedestrian traffic, provided for a front office design with a retail attitude. Commenting on this area, Pamela Meyer-Maynard, Director of Interior Design, explains, "It was important to create both a welcoming environment for our clients as well as a space that exposed the general public to the practice of architecture." Evoking both contemporary and modern design sensibilities, the bold use of materials and project imagery, combined with classic Eames furniture, serves to engage passersby.

The reception, waiting, and main conference areas open onto a central workspace, designed to provide for the ease of workflow and office communication. Low partitioned workstations are configured in a circular sweep against exterior window-walls.

date of completion	2001
number of employees	26
total square footage	8,000
number of conference rooms	3
typical workspace (average)	64 sf

1 Workarea
2 Graphics at Reception
3 Conference Room
4 Cafe & Material Library
5 Reception and Project Display

Photography Credits:
Ryan Beck and John Connell

At the center of the workstation arc is a multi-purpose open space that may be used for such ad hoc activities as project display and critique and whole-office gatherings.

Maple veneers and painted accent walls provide continuity and warmth throughout an office that features super-graphics, steel I-beam structures, exposed ductwork, and the extensive use of glass. Accent materials include stained MDF board, fiberglass panels, neon tubing, and exposed galvanized stud walls. The unique coffee bar/material library, with its feel of a small bookstore/cafe, provides a quiet oasis for employees within this dynamic office space.

4

3

5

Lavallee/Brensinger Architects

architecture
interior design
planning

29

Lavallee/Brensinger Architects occupy approximately one-eighth of a textile mill in the Amoskeag Millyard in Manchester, New Hampshire.

The mill building was chosen because of the strength of its architectural character, its generously proportioned space, and its location in the center city; it is the hope that this investment encourages further downtown revitalization.

The design aesthetic is a blend of the historic mill, as expressed through exposed masonry walls and timber columns, beams and deck, and "funky" modern industrial. One example is the new interior storefronts; assemblies of vertical iron "tees", between which stacked wooden storm windows are anchored with stainless carriage bolts. The storefronts add a sense of newness, while transparently preserving views to the historic structure; all through the use of appropriately "industrial" materials. It is such expression of both the contrast and compatibility of old and new, historic and modern, which energizes the resultant space and its enthusiastic users.

Floor Plan

date of completion	2001
number of employees	35
total square footage	8,600
number of conference rooms	4
typical workspace size	72 sf
custom workstations	yes

Photography Credits:
Joseph St. Pierre

6

5

7

8

9

10

Manasc Isaac Architects

2

30

1

Manasc Isaac Architects Ltd is an architecture firm located in Edmonton. The firm's renovated offices were completed in December of 2001. As a confirmed believer in sustainable design, MIA chose this forty year old structure with its narrow floor plate, with windows running the full length of the north and south sides.

Designed by partner Richard Isaac, the goal of the office's renovation was to allow for and encourage a free exchange of ideas among the staff. While risking the possibility of too much distraction and noise with the open floor plan, Richard has overcome this potential side effect with a better cross-fertilization of information. The workspaces for the principals of the firm are located centrally in the office and not in individual offices.

With the number of windows and the narrowness of the building, each person has natural light and natural ventilation. Most Edmonton offices have air conditioning, but MIA has chosen to decline this option and rely upon the natural ventilation and the heavy concrete structure to maintain a cool interior climate.

The existing suspended ceiling was removed to expose the concrete deck above and direct/indirect lighting was installed. This type of lighting reduced the number of fixtures by 50 to 60%, as the reflectivity of the ceiling increases the effectiveness of each fixture.

An administration island is located in the center of the space, containing all the files, plotters and printers, etc. Product literature is filed in the custom designed bookcases with standing height glass tops, which are used for drawing layout surfaces as well as a built-in light table.

The staff kitchen can also be called the design library. All design books and magazines are located in this space, along with a bar for eating lunch. This space is highly designed for entertaining clients and guests on a more informal basis.

3

date of completion	2001
number of employees	25
total square footage	8,400
number of conference rooms	2
typical workspace (average)	90 sf

5

1 Display
2 Logo
3 Reception
4 Floor Plan
5 Central Island
6 Typical Workstation
7 Lounge

Photography Credits:
Sonny Shem

6

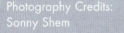

In addition to the architectural division of MIA, an industrial design company called d-lab started in the summer of 2001. Below the studio, the workshop area is used for the development and building of prototypes for elements which are used in architectural design and for marketed items such as display items, furniture and lighting. Product design is reflective in many areas throughout the office, as MIA was conscious of cost saving through the use of innovative design with inexpensive materials. The bookcases are made from clear finished MDF, the administration island is formed from industrial corrugated steel, the floors are natural clear concrete, and the ceilings are exposed painted concrete.

The final design displays an 'almost finished' appearance rather than a complete corporate image. The space offers many opportunities for future vertical elements, as well as volume to experiment with bold graphic ideas. The atmosphere is one which is lively and flexible as needs or mood dictate.

4

7

McCarty Holsaple McCarty

architecture
interior design

31

McCarty Holsaple McCarty, Inc. is an architecture and interior design firm located in downtown Knoxville, Tennessee. In the original office layout, there was a desire to create an open studio appearance, fostering team communication, visual unity, and work energy. Workstations are organized into two distinct rows, with a built-in hierarchy of station sizes. The main spine of workstations proceeds from the front end building facade to the river view facade along the studio spaces' central axis. A secondary visual axis is expressed from the elevator entry lobby to an open conference area. The perimeter of the open studio space has pockets of directors offices and conference areas, which are explicitly organized into a visually ordered bay system. This composition is illustrated in the regular arrangement of architectural columns, recessed glass walls, and projected solid partitions. Director's offices remain visually open with the use of full height semi-frosted glass partitions.

date of completion	1990
number of employees	34
total square footage	13,180
number of conference rooms	3
typical workspace (average)	56 sf

1 Exterior
2 Director's office
3 Reception
4 Director's Office
5 Office w/ Conference Area
6 Floor Plan
7 Director's Office

Photography Credits:
Robert Batey Photography

5

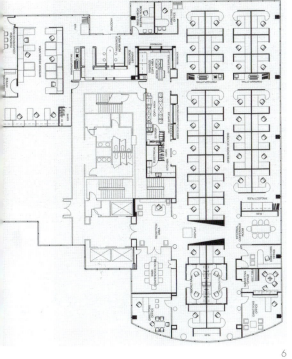

6

7

Norris Dullea

Norris Dullea is a planning and landscape architecture firm located in Denver, Colorado. The design and construction of the studios were realized over the course of several years. An existing historic brick warehouse structure was purchased and renovated. Due to subsequent growth of the organization, a few years later, the adjacent single story brick building was also acquired and renovated. The buildings share a common wall.

32

The concept for the original renovation was based on establishing several landmark architectural elements within the tall volume of the original building. These include a conference room, principals' offices, a wall along the public circulation route, a trellis above an informal meeting area, and a "tower" containing HVAC equipment and an administrator's office. These landmarks establish an identity and shape a space for a variety of functions, scale down the long narrow space, and provide the character of the space through a variety of materials and colors.

The original concept has been extended with the addition of more space and its subsequent renovations. In addition, a new architectural element was established to connect the two buildings — a long curved wall extending through the plan. The materials used in the construction of the wall reflect the connection between the earth and the professionals within the firm.

The wall begins in the original building as a steel frame with cedar plank open siding (similar to exterior wood fencing), continues into the new building, leaves a gap to allow passage to the office areas, and then begins again as a steel frame containing rocks (a similar construction technique used for retaining walls in landscaping projects). The wall then continues through a new window in the west wall of the building and extends eight feet into an exterior landscaped courtyard. This design element greets visitors arriving in central Denver via Colfax Avenue — the main east-west street of metropolitan Denver.

date of completion	2000
number of employees	44
total square footage	11,250
number of conference rooms	3
typical workspace (average)	70 sf

Architect:
Dan H. O'Brien
Photography Credits:
John Birkey, ASLA
Dan H. O'Brien

Office of Michael Rosenfeld

1

In 1983, The Office of Michael Rosenfeld, *Architects*, purchased a decommissioned Catholic church in the West Acton, Massachusetts historic district to house new studio space for the firm's architectural staff. The historic preservation/renovation occurred in three phases.

33

Phase one of construction divided the sanctuary into two separate levels to double the facility's amount of usable space. Offices in the former altar space are screened from the main studio space by an enclosed stair. A conference room located near the main entry separates the reception area from the rest of the first floor.

Phase two lowered the floor of the existing basement to create a lower level full of usable offices and a second conference room. New windows, placed in the stone foundation, flood the space with fresh air and natural daylight. A ramp from the parking lot creates barrier-free handicapped access.

The third and final phase transformed the upper level into a large, open studio. A long continuous roof ridge skylight runs the length of the roof to form a bright, naturally lit workplace. Morning and evening light filters through the original stained glass windows, located on the east and west facing walls, casting a beautiful spectrum of color across the space.

As OMR continued to grow, the company purchased and transformed a neighboring house into three more levels of studio and office space. A wooden terrace built around a large spruce tree connects the church with the new annex. The tree shelters the picnic tables of an outdoor meeting and gathering area.

Glass doors line the annex's ground floor walls to give the building a light, transparent feel. Offices surround a third conference room in the basement. Upstairs, a studio mimics the bright, open air of the upper level in the church building with skylights and natural lighting.

OMR developed its campus in the heart of a traditional New England village. In doing so, it purchased several neighboring buildings and possesses the ability to restore these structures should further expansion become necessary.

4

2

3

date of completion	1998
number of employees	44
total square footage	10,000
number of conference rooms	3
typical workspace	75 sf

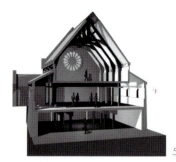

5

1   Building Exterior
2   Interior Window
3   Main Entry
4   Lock Detail
5   Before and After Section
6   Conference Room
7   Second Floor Studio/Work Area
8   Stair
9   Floor Plans

Photography Credits:
Lucy Goldstein
Derick Veliz

6

7

8

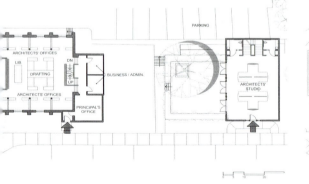

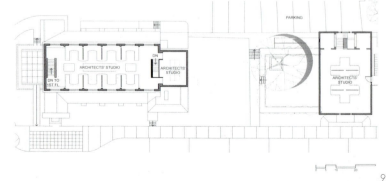

9

Semple Brown Design

2

34

Semple Brown Design, P.C. is a thirty person architecture and interior firm located in Denver, Colorado. The design priorities for the development of the 12,000 sf warehouse space, previously used as a local post office, were to redefine a pedestrian oriented street front; incorporate existing elements, such as the loading dock opening, into the design; as well as creating a 'community' working environment that infused creativity, inventiveness, and innovation.

The existing masonry shell of the building was retained as well as the precast concrete entry portal. A new ten foot by ten foot perforated steel 'garage' door serves as an entry gate and creates a canopy above the entry.

The space is oriented along a curving interior 'street', originating from the most public gathering point, the building entry, and continuing through the office, gently drawing one into the building. This interior 'street' intersects the exterior commercial street of Santa Fe Drive. At the building entry, three architectural masses, two conference rooms, and the reception desk, form the public node.

The two edges of the street are defined as extremes; the north edge by means of a relatively solid high-density particleboard wall, while the south edge is simply a three inch diameter pipe suspended at a ten foot height running continuously through the space. At the far end of the interior 'street', the existing

1

loading dock openings allow for natural lighting to flood the studio.

The loading dock was infilled to match the building's floor level; a concrete wall was placed on the south side to enclose the garden and create a noise barrier. The new concrete walls fall short of the full length of the building, adding depth to the street edge and allowing passersby to see the activity in the studio and the garden. The garden serves as an extension of the office, where employees are able to enjoy lunch and hold meetings.

The loading dock doors opening along the new garden were retained, with new steel frame storefronts added to each bay while the existing metal roll-down doors serve as window shutters on the interior of the space.

3

The addition furthers the 'extension' of the office and opens into the enclosed garden via a glass and aluminum overhead-rolling door. While being of a different vocabulary than the existing building, it maintains the same sense of simplicity. With framed walls, corrugated

date of completion	2000
number of employees	30
total square footage	12,000
number of conference rooms	5
typical workspace	80 sf

1 Exterior Detail
2 Interior Street
3 Garden Entry
4 Exterior Sunshading
5 Courtyard Nightscape

Photography Credits:
Ron Pollard Photography
Andrew Moss – Image 1

4

5

6   Design Studio
7   Diagram A
8   Diagram B
9   Reception/Lobby
10 Kitchen Screen
11 Lobby

metal deck, and sheet metal skin, the lunch/break room addition becomes the social center of the office as well as the physical connection between the interior and exterior.

The workstation system follows through with a language of planes. The entire system is flexible and able to be rearranged at any point. Workstation partitions consist of lightweight steel frames set on casters, each with two panels, a taller semi-transparent polygal, and a shorter medium density stained fiberboard adding a punch of color and order to the space.

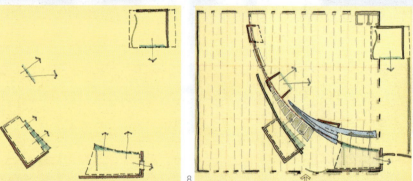

TRO/The Ritchie Organization

architecture
planning
engineering
interior design

- Reception / Gallery
- Multi-Purpose Areas
- Design Studio
- Conference Rooms
- Support Spaces

TRO/The Ritchie Organization, a four-office architectural/engineering firm, made use of the refurbished 1901 Goldsmith's Department Store building (now the Pembroke Building), utilizing the second floor, along with an attached vaulted contemporary infill space, for the relocation of its Memphis office.

35

Careful study was made to allow the preservation of this space's historic character and detail without compromising its modern function as a collaborative state-of-the-art design studio.

Contemporary Allsteel workstations from the Terrace Collection, with embossed metal clear coated panels, are interwoven in an open studio that is visually broken only by the original ornate plaster columns. By utilizing exposed mechanical, electrical and communications systems, the 14-foot ceilings and column capitals remain as important design elements. All principals and staff sit in open workstations, with the only private offices belonging to accounting and network support personnel.

date of completion	2002
number of employees	35
total square footage	14,000
number of conference rooms	5
typical workspace size	74 sf

Photography Credits:
© 2002 Jeffrey Jacobs/Architectural
Photography Inc.
Memphis, Tennessee

The reception desk was sanded to provide a unique swirled design in the metal. This design is echoed in the swirled carpet pattern of the Gallery, which flanks the open studio and guides visitors to conference and gathering spaces, allowing glimpses into the studio as well as displays of projects in progress. Sliding perforated metal display panels were specially designed so project boards of any size could be hung using a nut and bolt system.

Original large bay windows provide sunlight and additional space for sitting. Contemporary lighting elements blend seamlessly with traditional finishes such as the historic pressed tin ceiling. Exposed brick and plaster walls are juxtaposed against the simple, sophisticated rectangular carpet pattern in the high-tech conference rooms.

Further emphasizing the firm's values, TRO made use of local artisans to assist in providing contemporary details that harmonize with the historic fabric of the space. To separate the reception area from the large, open studio, dividers were created from sanded plexiglass, creating a frosted appearance, and hung by regular hardware. The cleanness and simplicity are stunning, while being extremely functional. This method was also utilized at windows in the Gallery to shield harsh sunlight.

4

5 Design Studio
6 Light Detail
7 High-tech Conference Room
8 Gallery

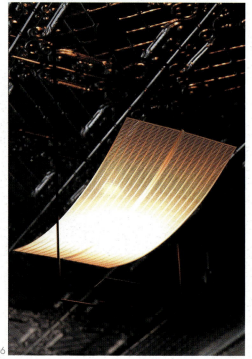

Tuck · Hinton Architects

architecture

2

Tuck Hinton Architects is a full service design firm located in Nashville, Tennessee. The firm's offices relocated in 1995 to the historic 1860 Elm Street United Methodist Church, which is on the Historic Register. This was the first rehabilitation in Nashville of a large downtown church into a 12,000 sf architectural studio.

36

The church's beautiful steeple burned in the 1920s and was never rebuilt. After having one of the largest Sunday School attendances in the area in the 1940s, the city's population began shifting to the suburban areas and took a toll on the Elm Street's membership until 1971 when it closed. As the city grew, the neighborhoods surrounding Elm Street became commercial and industrialized. Following the closing of Elm Street, the features of value were stripped from the building and sold for salvage. The stained glass windows and railing around the sanctuary were sold to TGI Friday's Restaurant, which recouped the purchaser's entire investment in the building and property. The pipe organ, thought to be the first in Nashville, and other finery, are also now gone.

In the late 1970s, a previous owner stabilized the deteriorating and abandoned structure. PMT Services occupied the building in the 1980s. In 1994, Tuck Hinton Architects purchased the church and performed a major restructuring and reconfiguration of the interior spaces to accommodate the firm's growing needs.

After nearly 140 years, the northeast altar wall of the sanctuary began to settle and shift outward. To stabilize the corner, a concrete buttress was erected and topped with a 'protector' gargoyle named ''Doggett'', after the Bishop Doggett, who consecrated the church in the 1870s.

3

1

date of completion	1995
number of employees	20
total squae footage	12,000
number of conference rooms	4
typical workspace	100 sf

7

8

1 Buttress w/ Gargoyle
2 Renovated Front Facade
3 Building Sections
4 Interior Project Display
5 Original Church Structure
6 Studio
7 Stairway
8 Candlelit Interior
9 Floor Plans
10 Exterior Window Detail

Photography Credits:
Kem Hinton

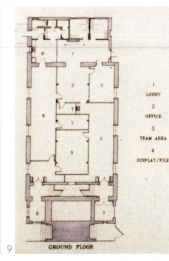

LOBBY

OFFICE

TEAM AREA

DISPLAY/FILE

CONFERENCE

REFERENCE

FILE

BREAK

9   GROUND FLOOR   MAIN FLOOR   BALCONY

6

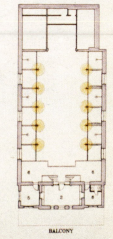

5

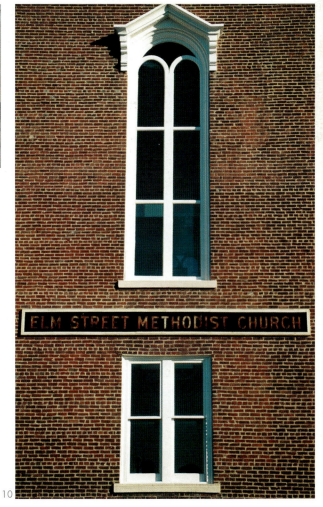

ELM STREET METHODIST CHURCH

10

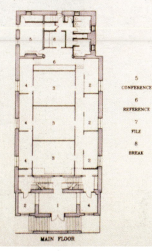

Witsell Evans Rasco

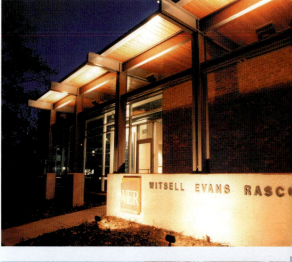

2

37

WER's architectural office is housed in a renovated 1963 Studebaker showroom located in downtown Little Rock.

The street presence was enhanced by constructing a new canopy that provided shelter, decorative lighting, and signage to better define the entrance. Additional space behind the studio, currently occupied by a separate tenant, can be utilized for future expansion.

The existing restrooms, breakroom, and mechanical spaces were retained as a common area for both tenants. The conference room was kept transparent to the studio and doubles as a display and presentation area, with tackable wall panels and a projection wall.

The clear span structure was utilized for an open atmosphere studio, taking advantage of the original showroom's exposure to north light.

3

W·E·R
ARCHITECTS/PLANNERS

date of completion	2000
number of employees	20
total square footage	5,000
number of conference rooms	2
typical workspace (average)	72 sf

1 Reception
2 Entry
3 Exterior at Night
4 Floor Plan
5 Studio
6 Conference Room
7 Display at Entry

Photography Credits:
Matt Bradley

4

IZARD STREET

BNIM Architects

architecture
interior design
sustainable
design

1

BNIM Architects, an architectural and interior design firm, occupies three-and-one-half floors of the Power and Light Building in downtown Kansas City. With over thirty-three years of experience and projects that advance the state of art and the environment, BNIM Architects is an established design presence, entrusted with many significant public and private building projects at both local and national levels.

38

The past seventy years had taken a toll on the Power and Light Building's impressive two-story lobby space. Once graceful Corinthian columns and delicately carved plaster walls had begun to crumble and developed gaping holes. A local artist and plaster contractor collaborated with BNIM to determine how each of the areas would be replaced or restored. Molds were created of existing ornate plaster sections, while the large stone block motif on the walls was restored by hand using a scribing technique. A local painter applied silver leafing with layers of green, red and orange glazes to accentuate the sunburst and lightning bolt art deco motifs.

BNIM's renovated office space set the example for revitalizing one of the most prestigious Art Deco buildings in the nation and a treasure of Kansas City architecture. The firm's state-of-the-art furnishings and fixtures emphasize the historical richness of the building. This interplay between old and new led BNIM to restore to its original splendor the lobby and second floor mezzanine. The result is a flexible space where travertine marble, silver-leaf stucco and rare nickel-silver railings blend with translucent glass, ergonomic stations and wireless technology conceived for the design laboratory of the future.

BNIM researched each of the following issues in terms of advancing a sustainable community site selection, focusing on urban development, salvaging of existing materials for reuse or donation to local agencies, materials concerning energy efficiency, human and environmental health, durability and performance, resource limitation, waste management and flexibility with the use of systems furniture.

2

date of completion	2000
number of employees	100
total square footage	27,000
number of conference rooms	8
typical workspace size	80 sf
manufactured workstations	yes

1 Conference Room
2 Front Elevation
3 Office 8x11
4 Studio

BNIM's renovation of three floors of this historic landmark demonstrates a commitment to the revitalization of the urban core. Display windows showcase the work of local artists.

The dynamic studio workspace is characterized by layers of visual overlap between the restored first and second levels.

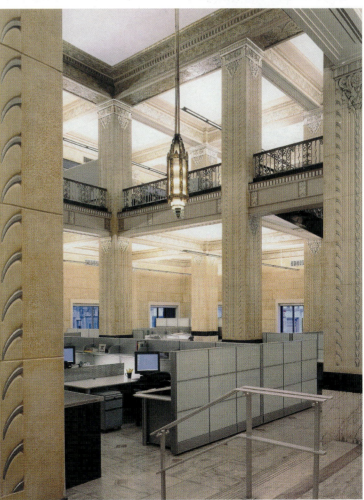

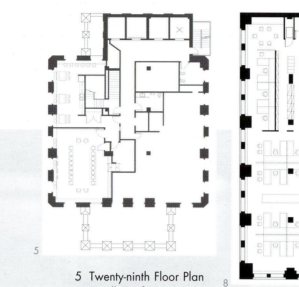

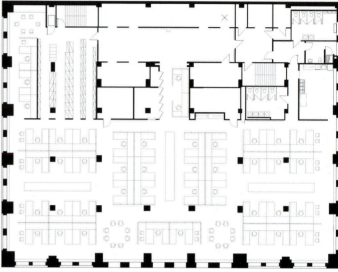

5 Twenty-ninth Floor Plan
6 Small Conference Areas
7 Studio
8 Third Floor Plan
9 Second Floor Plan
10 First Floor Plan
11 Reception/Gallery

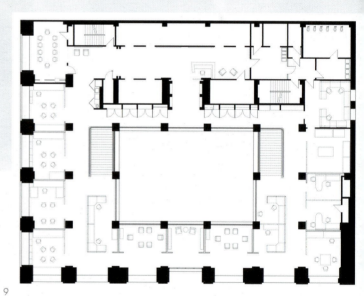

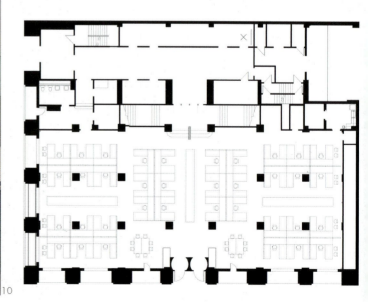

Centerbrook Architects & Planners

architecture
planning
interiors

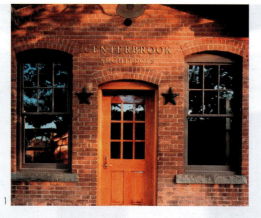

1

Centerbrook is an architecture and planning firm established in 1975. Located in a renovated mill building on the Falls River in the village of Centerbrook, Connecticut, the firm has two principals, five partners, and a staff of eighty.

Centerbrook traces its roots to architect Charles W. Moore, who assumed the position of Dean at the Yale School of Architecture in 1965. Moore founded Charles W. Moore Associates that year in New Haven. Within five years the firm had outgrown cramped quarters across the street from the architecture school and decided to move to a spacious, nineteenth century mill building in Centerbrook, Connecticut. A factory in the building had made drill bits for nearly 100 years, much of the time powered by the Falls River.

Over the years, Centerbrook rented space throughout the complex to many different tenants ranging from an antiques dealer to a saw sharpener, sculptors, a furniture stripper, interior decorators, moccasin maker, a gift shop, lawyers, art consultants, graphic designers, psychiatrists, massage therapist, and writers.

The Union Hall building, next to the mill building, was Charles Moore's residence for a few years. Today, it is joined to the mill building and serves as the conference room for staff training programs, office meetings, and client meetings.

It is the firm's largest meeting room, holding up to eighty people.

A flood in June 1982 caused significant changes to the appearance of the property. Fourteen inches of rain in twenty-four hours caused the Falls River to rise up and take away six buildings. The main buildings were saved from being undermined by a stone tunnel, which is the headrace for the hydropower plant.

It took more than a year and a Federal Disaster Loan to repair the damage. The result turned out to be a great improvement over the earlier shabbier look of the place. The rentable floor area was increased by making the one-story 'Forge' building into a two-story building for offices and connecting it to the adjoining buildings by indoor and outdoor bridges. The waterworks below the dam were rebuilt in 1983 to prevent future flood damage, and the new Forge building, now called the "Gold Coast", was elevated on concrete piers above the predicted flood height.

Today Centerbrook occupies almost the entire complex of 20,000 square feet. The offices are laid out in an open office plan. All architects, including partners, sit in work spaces of roughly the same size. This allows for a free exchange of ideas and conversation.

39

date of completion	n/a
number of employees	80
total square footage	20,000
number of conference rooms	4
typical workspace (average)	50 sf

1 Entrance on Main Street
2 Roof-top Deck overlooking Falls
  River
3 Aerial View

Photography Credits:
Timothy Hursley 1,4,5,8,10
Robert Benson 6,7
Don Couture 3
Centerbrook Architects 2

2

3

5

4

4 Upper Drafting Room
5 Upper Level of Lobby
6 Falls River
7 Falls River and Dam with two-story ''Gold Coast''
8 Aluminum ''paper airplane'' protecting entrance to ''Gold Coast'' on left and Mill Building to right
9 Floor Plans
10 Main Street with ''Union Hall'' at left and Factory Building to right

6

7

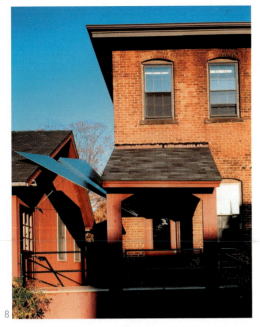

8

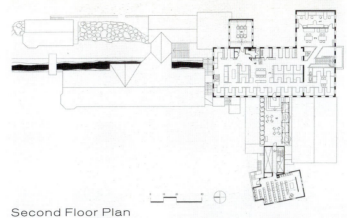

Second Floor Plan

First Floor Plan

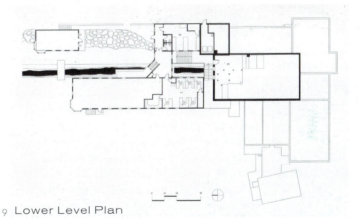

9 Lower Level Plan

Conference Room." There are also a variety of other spaces for informal gatherings and smaller meetings. These include the Drill Bit Gallery, used for art exhibits; the Ping Pong Room, for the annual tournament; the "Loft," with two tables of four for small meetings; a coffee bar with large table, refrigerator, and the microwave that is used for lunches and meetings; and a roof deck overlooking the Falls River.

The Falls River hydropower plant, repaired after the flood, continues to make about 24,000 kwh each year.

10

D'Adda, Lorenzini, Vigorelli, BBDO

1

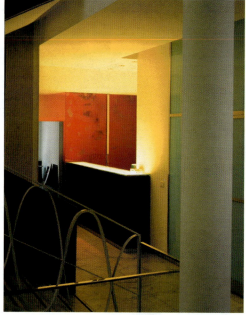

2

40

Morality apart, making images that transcend those we already know seems to be what advertisers and interior designers have in common. Making people understand that an ordinary four-walled box can fly – albeit architecturally important respectfully preserved, as here is the same as making people believe that any given product can change their lives, even if the truth of the first proposition is entirely self-evident, and of the second entirely debatable. Be this as it may, UdA has really succeeded in making the interior design of the building match the kind of work that is done in it.

Taking enlarged, interchangeable, backlighted, decontextualised images and turning them into walls means transforming the routine of work into a dream of what that work can achieve. Such shifts or accentuations of meaning occur frequently in the work of Camagna, Camoletto, Marcante (UdA). Examples here range from the enhancement of purely "service" elements (otherwise merely functional see-through closets that are backlighted to reveal the outlines of clothes and objects), the creation of memorable scenes in makeshift spaces (temporariness becomes an event, in the form of a projection, synchronised with the lighting system, of slides in a rented house), and the use of materials normally employed for other purposes or to create other images (river pebbles, certain "Ruhulmann" woods and, in parallel, semi-finished products typical of

Turin's mechanical engineering industry). In the D'Adda, Lorenzini, Vigorelli, BBDO advertising agency, the departure from normal house design, acceptance of the challenge posed by architecture as outstanding as Asnago and Vender's, enables the firm to assess more accurately an important aspect of UdA's work, namely its carefully contrived balance between the need to intervene (whence the recognisability, and therefore, uniqueness, of the result) and the need to play an essentially background role. This is a lesson for interior designers and there are many in the field of office design who think that a designed interior should be a kind of camouflage that more or less conceals what really goes on in the office, but is in fact boringly uniform and totally indifferent to the architectural context in which it is sited.

date of completion	1998
number of employees	60
total square meters	1500
number of conference rooms	2
typical workspace	20

1 Reception/Lobby
2 Reception Desk
3 Seating Area
4 Conference Room

Architect:
UdA (Walter Camagna,
Massimiliano Camoletto,
Andrea Marcante)
Photography Credits:
Mario Ermoli
Text by permission:
Modified from Marco Romanelli
article for ABITARE magazine

3

4

5 Stairway
6 Screenwalls
7 First Floor Plan
8 Ground Floor Plan
9 Basement Plan
10 Sections
11 Enlarged, Backlit Walls

7

8

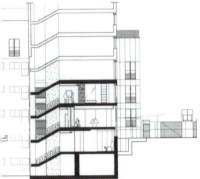

10

9

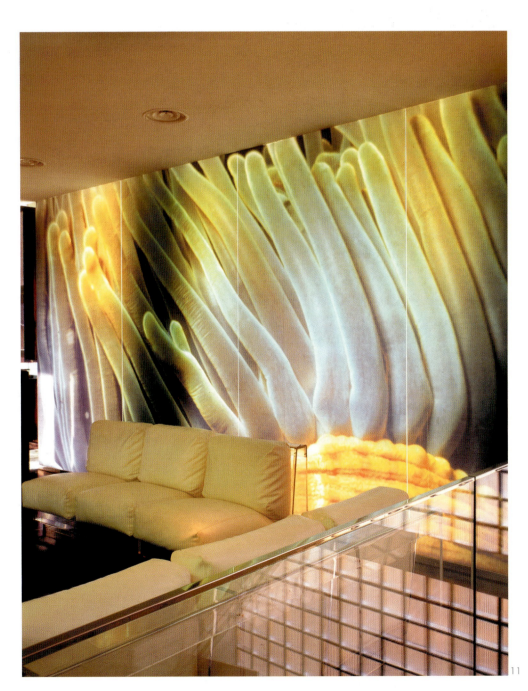

11

Flad & Associates

41

In 1995, the Flad & Associates staff took residence in their new facility located in Madison, Wisconsin. The architecture, engineering, planning and interiors firm established a primary goal for this new facility – to design an environment which fully supports the mission of creating environments that enhance human potential. That mission was to be conveyed visually in a welcoming atmosphere – an environment that stimulated creativity and communication, facilitated multi-disciplined project teams and represented visually the firm's philosophy.

Planning an environment that would facilitate teamwork and interaction was also paramount and, as a result, the building has a very simple interior plan and exterior expression. A contemporary 'loft space,' the building design communicates the technological focus and houses multiple teams of people working interactively on a variety of projects at any one time.

The architectural, structural, mechanical, and lighting systems are exposed and integrated into the building's design. An acoustical deck, combined with a carpeted floor, results in a very quiet acoustical environment. Fixed offices are concentrated on the southern side of the building, and open team spaces are located to the north along a full glazed wall to maximize light flow into the building interior without glare. This fully glazed wall provides panoramic views of the beautiful prairie beyond. An interconnecting stair and a centralized reception and resource area which is the 'heart' of the building encourage frequent interaction and communication within the office.

date of completion	1995
number of employees	300
total square footage	56,000
number of conference rooms	10
typical workspace size	54/81sf

1 North Elevation
2 East Elevation
3 Reception (Beyond)
 Product Library (Below)
4 Team Collaboration Space

3

2

4

5 Workstations
6 Reception
7 Design Studio

5

6

Hassell

1

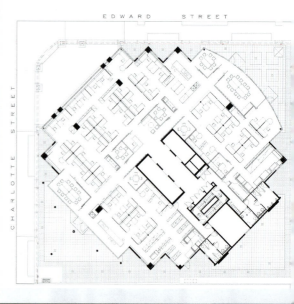

EDWARD STREET

CHARLOTTE STREET

2

42

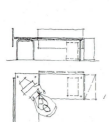

The main focus of the HASSELL brief was to create an environment that reflected the importance of transparency between all individuals involved in the design process. The firm wanted to design an interior fitout that generated an open, inviting workplace that encouraged a strong collaborative working relationship between client and staff. The new HASSELL office resides in Australia's first highrise building to employ energy conservation design principles. This theme was continued and includes the key concepts of clarity and strength that are embodied in the design of the new offices in the Hall Chadwick Centre.

3

The structural and material aspects of the fitout glass, steel and white plasterboard planes, generate an open accessible client/ staff facility. The interaction of exterior and interior spaces is heightened through the use of transparent, reflective materials where the terraces become an extension of the office environment rather than the precious occasional use spaces. In addition, they form part of the ESD agenda, providing Staff and Clients with an opportunity to step outside and enjoy the city. The firm developed a custom work module to respond to the level of flexibility required by a multidisciplinary design practice. Generous in footprint, the work module consists of desks sliding and locking on a rail

date of completion   2001
number of employees   62
total square footage   62
number of conference rooms   7

124

Photography Credits:
Tony Phillips 4
Vincent Long 1, 7, 8
David Sandison 3, 5, 9, 10, 11

4

system for ease of configuration. Visual access from the workpoint is maintained through a minimum use of screening. The reticulation of services is through an umbilical as an alternative to full height, solid elements. Furthermore, the traditionally hidden away staff facility 'the tea room', is brought into the work environment, fostering multi-discipline collaboration and social connection to facilitate the transparency process.

For HASSELL one of the issues was creating transparent and open spaces that still enabled some level of privacy. The open tea benches positioned at the extents of work areas facilitate informal meeting areas appropriate for both staff and clients. Glass meeting rooms positioned along the main street are designed for small meetings with the main boardroom positioned at the end axis to incorporate the outdoor area.

The mix of rubber flooring and carpet enables acoustic privacy to adjacent workstations. Only one meeting room consists of full height plasterboard walls with large sliding timber panels that are left open when the meeting room is not in use to allow optimum levels of natural light and return the space to the desired level of transparency.

5

6

7 Reception
8 Tea Station
9 Studio
10 Exterior View
11 Glazing Detail

The fitout cost was checked against the initial budget to ensure a cost effective outcome for the project. As the project budget was finite, HASSELL rigorously researched cost effective and sustainable products and materials. A significant example of this is the use of recycled rubber flooring to define the main axis/street of the office. The fitout uses T5 fluorescent lighting and low flow hydraulics, both cost effective alternatives to standard fluorescent lamps and hydraulic systems. HASSELL developed a flexible and cost effective work module based on UNI-SYSTEM TABLE DESKING. By adding a customised perforated metal screen and power reticulation, each workpoint at the outset priced significantly lower per workpoint than a standard workstation system. The Uni-System Table is also used in meeting rooms and the workstation environment, which are interchangeable to increase flexibility. Furthermore, churn costs are greatly reduced as it is extremely simple to reconfigure.

9

10

11

The office spaces flow from the main axis and street linking the two outdoor terraces. From this axis, open links were maintained that allow easy flow between the different workspaces. Built up elements are confined to the building core but still maintain some transparency and flexibility. The use of glass, steel and unadorned plasterboard planes, maximises flexibility, transparency and a sense of space responding to the conceptual strategy. ESD principals played a role in the design and selection of materials. Advantage was taken wherever possible of the early works and opportunities available as the building was being constructed.

LandDesign

land planning
site development
engineering
surveying

1

2

43

LandDesign, Inc. began in 1977, in Charlotte, North Carolina as a company specializing in site planning and landscape design. It has grown and evolved over the years and today provides a fully integrated range of services including land planning, site development and engineering services from its seven office locations. These seven offices employ over one hundred and sixty professionals.

LandDesign has won more than thirty professional awards from national and state organizations.

Vision Statement

Retain and restore the character of the historic industrial building while also expanding upon its original size, through the addition of floors.

Blend the historic nature of the building with the company's innovative approach to design through an opening, inviting, and flexible space that fosters creativity and adapts to the needs of the growing company.

Convey character through rich materials that refer to nature through color, texture, and shape.

3

date of completion	2001
number of employees	55
total square footage	25,136
number of conference rooms	4
typical workspace size	63 sf
custom workstations	yes

5

1 Building Facade
2 Entry Stair
3 Conference Room
4 Elevator Lobby Reception Desk
5 Studio and Offices
6 Main Reception Desk
7 Typical Workstation

Photography Credits:
LandDesign

6

4

7

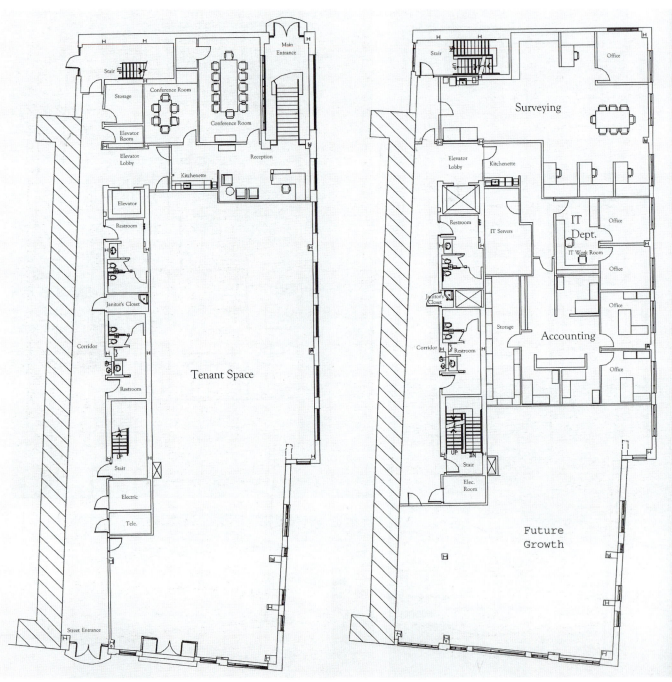

First Floor

Second Floor

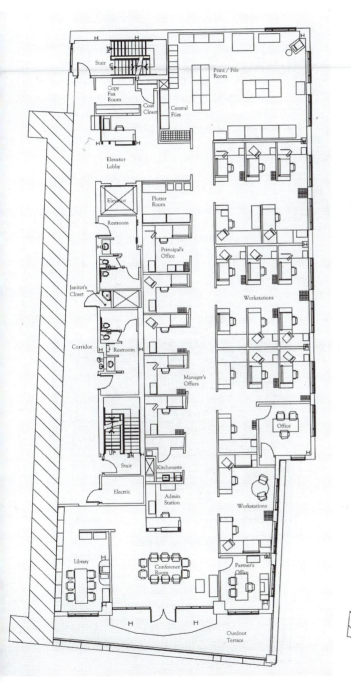

Third Floor

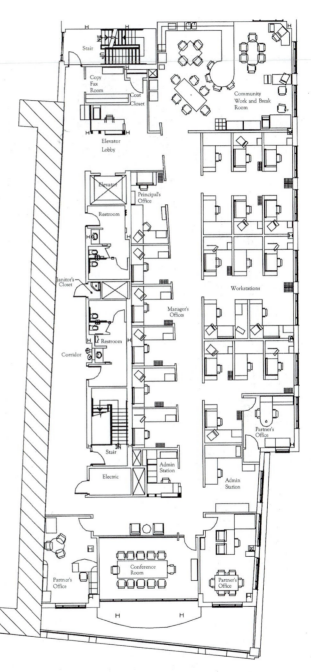

Fourth Floor

Looney Ricks Kiss

1

44

Looney Ricks Kiss Architects, a 116 person design firm headquartered in Memphis, Tennessee, with additional offices in Nashville, Princeton, and Celebration, Florida, rose to the design opportunity for the preservation and renovation of the historical Toyota Center. Completed in September 2000, this eight-story, 200,000 sf historical rehabilitation/renovation of the William R. Moore Drygoods Building brings life to the original 1913 structure. In 1982, the structure was included in the National Register of Historic Places. This early example of cast-in-place concrete construction was vacated in 1986 and received no maintenance for over twelve years. As an integral element of the Memphis ballpark development, the building was rehabilitated for critical operating functions required by the ballpark. Sited adjacent to AutoZone Park's entry plaza, it houses the ballpark catering kitchen, the Memphis Redbirds team offices, a private stadium club, and a ballpark retail store. It also provides Class A office space for Looney Ricks Kiss, the Memphis Grizzlies, and other companies.

Rehabilitation was performed on the primary facades, with the ground and second floor completely restored. All original columns throughout the building remain fully exposed in the office and corridor spaces. The tenant spaces are designed with a warehouse-type floor plate with open office environments, exposed columns and ceiling structure. A raised pedestrian bridge on the secondary facade links the various service areas of the building to the ballpark while meeting the preservation requirements. A portion of the glazed area on the upper four floors has been enlarged with floor-to-ceiling glass to maximize the views into the ballpark from the corporate meeting rooms. As a piece of this design opportunity, LRK became a part of this downtown revitalization project.

2

date of completion	2000
number of employees	116
total square footage	37,852
number of conference rooms	21
typical workspace (average)	102 sf

1 Exterior
2 View of Stadium
3 Studio
4 Reception
5 Product Library

Photography Credits:
Jeffrey Jacobs/Architectural
Photography, Inc. Image #1

Scott McDonald —
Hedrich Blessing Photographers
Images #2-5, 8-10

4

3

The Looney Ricks Kiss open design studio on the 5th and 6th floors promotes interaction, enhances teamwork, and provides a collaborative work environment. An open monumental stair, linking the two floors, provides ample space at the top and bottom in the form of "porches," which offer homey, comfortable seating for impromptu discussions and more casual meetings. A symbolic climbing wall, next to the monumental stair, is a reminder for employees of their participation in a three-day off-site experiential learning retreat and ropes course called "One Firm Learning." A basketball hoop on the 5th floor and a "putting green" on the 6th floor, along with wider and irregular-shaped corridors and centralized coffee/mailbox areas, emphasize the social aspects of work. Client conference rooms are located near the reception area and elevator lobbies and have large windows that offer spectacular views of the LRK-designed AutoZone Park. Private phone booths are conveniently located outside the conference rooms. Non-client conference areas are located within the design studios and include open, flexible meeting spaces.

6 Fifth Floor
7 Sixth Floor
8 Columns
9 Porch Space
10 Climbing Wall

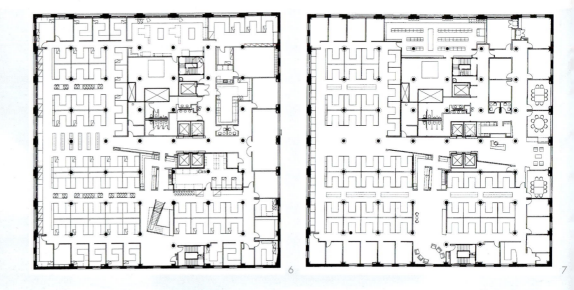

Marc-Michaels

interior design

45

Marc-Michaels Interior Design, Inc. is a design firm located in Winter Park, Florida. Designed to meet the growing needs of the firm, this office building was created to satisfy the current owner's needs. Featuring the latest in security, fire safety, and floor plan flexibility, the office space design was driven by the need to have plenty of storage for source materials used by the firm. Due to the size of the lot, the architect was restricted in the number of employee offices the building could contain and square footage. By adding a third-floor catwalk, the owner's storage needs were met without exceeding square footage limitations. Built-in bookcases line both sides of the catwalk, providing plenty of organized storage. Windows on each side of the building allow plenty of natural light for the open source room below.

date of completion	1998
number of employees	75
total square footage	11,372
number of conference rooms	2
typical workspace (average)	135 sf

Photography Credits:
Kim Sargent
Sargent Architectural Photography

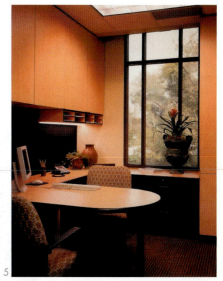

4

5

6

The reception area features a curved desk and credenza built out of maple with a mahogany finish and a breche de vendome marble top. The company's signature, carved stone medallion is centered above the cabinets. The Inca gold flooring is set on a diagonal with onyx mosaics laid in an exaggerated grid pattern, intersected by red onyx pin dots. The walls were treated with applied cut paper in a block pattern. Hand carved limestone columns were set in opposing corners to anchor the furnishings.

Wood panels line the walls of the two owner's offices. One is designed in a traditional form with dark stained maple woodwork. The other office is more reminiscent of an 'Armani' retail store. Clear, finished maple, with stainless steel reveals detail the cabinetry on each side of the office. Secondary offices feature a less expensive solution with melamine cabinetry in lieu of stained wood built-ins.

The conference room features a built-in buffet, which contains the sound system for the room. A plasma television is placed above the teleconferencing capabilities. This room also features raffia walls, limestone columns, stained trim, and sisal flooring.

PAVLIK Design Team

46

The PAVLIK Design Team is a full-service architectural and interior design organization founded in 1969. The firm is a team of passionate professionals headquartered in Fort Lauderdale, Florida, with joint venture offices in Tokyo, Osaka, Seoul, Buenos Aires, Sao Paulo, and Mexico City.

When designing the offices, the one thing that was taken into consideration was the firm's process beginning with an intensive exchange of information. In this phase, roles were defined as well as responsibilities, solidified schedules and indepth conduct discussions to be sure that everyone had the same objective and shared the same vision.

The firm is composed of one main building (three levels) and four (4) free standing houses, which take up one city block, each housing a particular discipline; the four houses have been an addition to the original design, but have worked for the benefit to better structure the firm.

Project teams are set up depending on the client's challenges; typically there are five to eight creative players per project (one or two players per discipline).

Each particular building/discipline has been identified through the use of the following colors: White, Blue, Red, Green, and Yellow. These unique colors create a definite identity/ icon which further identifies the PAVLIK DESIGN TEAM as: Passionate, creative, global, spirited, bold, innovative, and unique.

All furniture within the interior spaces has been custom designed to meet the needs and the color palette was carefully selected to maintain a clean, fresh, and inviting work environment. This was accomplished through the use of high whites, warm grays and satin-brushed metal accents.

date of completion	1980
number of employees	105
total square footage	10,000
number of conference rooms	4
typical workspace (average)	81 sf

1 Freestanding Houses
2 Yellow House - Printing
3 Main Building - Design and Production
4 Red House - Code and Materials
5 Blue House - Yacht

Photography Credits:
PAVLIK Design Team

3

4

5

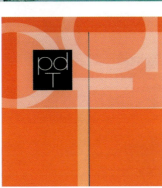

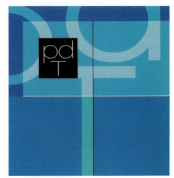

Pollard Thomas & Edwards

2

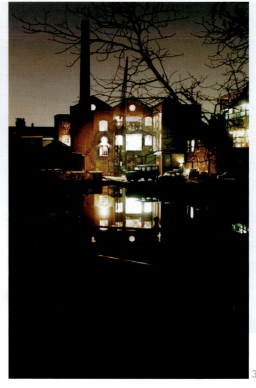

47

3

4

Diespeker Wharf is both a lovely place to work and an inspiring piece of urban regeneration. The restoration of an old timber wharf beside the Regent's Canal has created a tranquil enclave to counteract the stress of very busy and technologically orientated working patterns.

As much has been achieved by the removal of unnecessary things as by the addition of new.

The kinds of spaces that have resulted from Pollard Thomas & Edwards Architects' subtle realization of the development potential of the building and its site include:

– A canalside garden with a circular wisteria-screened external conference room

– An 'operations room' capable of being occupied by a team for blitzing interactive work to deadlines, such as competitions and exhibitions. It is technologically flexible and functions as a demountable studio, with stunning canal views and calm and creative ambience.

– A rooftop terrace suitable for an overstretched 'hermit' to opt out of the office environment.

1

date of completion	2000
number of employees	70
total square feet	8370
number of conference rooms	2
typical workspace (average)	46 sf

5

— Light airy 'loft' studio spaces which combine the workmanlike feel of the warehouse with cool modern interventions, such as the sliding glass screens in the old hoist door openings.

— A conference room sitting right next to the water, where the more intensive meetings can be alleviated by watching the heron fishing.

The building functions as a creative studio and a business space. It is occupied by two firms of architects and a head-hunting company which recruits executives (all job-seekers arrive for interview by chauffer).

6

The building combines the best use of existing structure with modern additions. The restored crane, for example, sits next to a glazed 'box' clad with thin cedar mullions.

The philosophy of the restoration has been to touch the existing fabric lightly — keeping the tough character of the original — and adding in appropriate new (light fittings made from cable trays, a conference table from industrial flooring grillage, simple sheets of glass hung from wheels).

The building is only now complete after a carefully phased programme over several years. It has however already picked up several awards and is featured regularly in Open House. Where there was previously an eyesore, PTE have acquired, developed, designed, and effected a transformation into one of the best office environments in Islington.

7

8

RTKL

1

RTKL is one of the world's leading multidisciplinary design firms, with an international portfolio of award-winning office, mixed use, retail/entertainment, hotel/resort, residential, health, and public projects. Today, RTKL's philosophy is practiced by more than 700 professionals, working in London, Tokyo, Hong Kong, Madrid, Chicago, Washington D.C., Los Angeles, Dallas, Baltimore, Denver, and Miami. RTKL is currently ranked by World Architecture as the 7th largest architecture firm in the world.

48

The Dallas office faced numerous challenges in designing their new facilities in the downtown Dallas Republic Bank Center. For years, the Republic complex, designed in 1954 by Harrison and Abromovitz of New York, stood as one of the quintessential modernist structures found in downtown Dallas. The original banking hall, with its refined aluminum curtain wall, column-free two-story space, terrazzo floors, maple paneled walls, white marble clad columns, and 250 foot long undulating gold leaf balcony, represented the best of post war era design. Upon discovering the vacated space, RTKL moved quickly to secure the location and design their new 60,000 sf Dallas home.

The concept capitalizes on the opportunity to use the design of their new space as an expression of the firm's core cultural values and philosophies, and to create the feeling of a studio setting. RTKL's solution is based on the architectural language found in the original space. To the general public, the space is eye

candy; rich in textures, crisp shapes and industrial lighting that make the space come alive. To clients, it is a visual representation of the firm's creativity in adaptive reuse. The design approach was to strip the original space down to its bare soul, and juxtapose new interventions with bold and refined elements. Utilizing color, platonic forms and material texture as visual codes/clues, the three-level offices unfold as visitors walk through the space. With the basic palette of terrazzo, white marble, gold leaf, aluminum, and exposed concrete found in the original space left intact, the new objects are juxtaposed with bold and more contemporary imagery such as maple for added warmth.

2

date of completion	2000
number of employees	151
total square footage	60,000
number of conference rooms	16
typical workspace	70 sf

Photography Credits:
RTKL Associates
Craig Blackmon
Turner Construction
Paul M. Schiefer

7

8

9

10

11

12

A clear stained maple wall panel system wraps over the existing grand stair through a large circular opening, and a new perforated, aluminum-clad elevator tower brings visitors up into the studio space. A bold red terrazzo floor demarks areas once occupied by an escalator in the original banking hall. A brushed zinc wall connects both ends of the ground floor lobby, acts as a foreground wall for their new conference facilities, and marks entry to their space by slicing through the street entry curtain wall. A series of colored waxed plaster finished walls add a new sense of depth and layering to spaces, and in turn helps define both circulation as well as boundaries. A crisp angled wall cuts through the gold leaf balcony, creating a central critique area, and new staircase.

The two-story wall also visually breaks up the dense workstation-filled environment. Senior staff offices mixed with project design rooms called "labs", which are color coded and built behind a Mondrian-inspired curtain wall system, flank the studio area.

RTKL's new offices are like a small coded urban space, with areas to rest and observe as well as areas to work and assemble. The general public is exposed to the firm's inner workings with conference rooms and window display space adjacent to the street. RTKL's new offices represent the new urban landscape. And, like all great urban landscapes, they require several visits to fully appreciate all the subtle nuances found in the spaces.

SWA Group, Sausalito

landscape
architecture
planning
urban design

1

2

49

SWA Group is a multidisciplinary firm in landscape architecture, urban design, and planning. The company is an offspring of the Bauhaus movement and, since its inception in 1957, it embraces the philosophy of collaborative practice. Through collaboration, each individual's strengths make up the greater whole, where the final built work reinforces the original "big idea".

Situated across the Golden Gate Bridge in Sausalito, the firm benefits from the entrepreneurial spirit and creativity of San Francisco, while finding the beauty of natural systems and personal fitness in Marin County an indispensable part of the practice.

Indoor Spaces:
The open space system fosters spontaneous discussion and team camaraderie between staff and principals. Within this larger open framework, smaller spaces are carved out based on building layout. The "fishbowl" is the central open space, with a 24' high ceiling; the "pukas" at building corners have 4' high walls for project displays; the mezzanines provide long views of the Sausalito marina. Abundant natural light, views and access into the gardens from workspaces are indispensable parts of the landscape practice.

3

date of completion	1970
number of employees	52
total square meters	14,000
number of conference rooms	2
typical workspace (average)	250 sf

1 Front Entrance
2 Demonstation Garden
3 Conference Room
4 Reception
5 Walls as pin-up space
6 Mezzanine
7 "Puka"

Photographers:
Tom Fox and Ying-Yu Hung

6

4

5

7

13

12

14

Outdoor Spaces:
While the indoor spaces promote open communication, the outdoor spaces are structured for many uses.

1. flexible space for material exploration, experimentation, and demonstration;
2. working space for real size mock up of landscape elements and paving samples;
3. garden space for testing new plant species;
4. spill out space for firm-wide meetings and Friday "hooch";
5. lawn court for ball games;
6. intimate space for contemplation and one-on-one conversation.

15

Zimmer Gunsul Frasca

architecture
interior design
urban planning

50

After years of incremental growth that resulted in a segregated workplace, the opportunity arose to relocate Zimmer Gunsul Frasca Partnership's (ZGF) Los Angeles office into a space that would bring the entire staff of 70 together – a space that would reflect the ideals of environmental responsibility and building community that inform all of the firm's architecture. The goal was to create an uplifting, sustainable environment for staff and visitors that would stimulate the imagination.

The selected space, 22,769-square-feet of the 37th floor in a downtown high-rise, was chosen for its high ceilings and few structural obstacles. The particular floor is located directly beneath a mechanical level in the building, accounting for the 18-foot floor-to-ceiling height. Thirteen-foot high windows around the office perimeter offer spectacular views and the advantage of keeping the staff connected with the city.

Beginning with a loft or warehouse concept, the design team created a space that is part laboratory of ideas and part gallery of completed design – juxtaposing raw and industrial elements with warm woods and bright colors in a sustainable setting. Much like an urban environment, the space functions as a community in the way the systems are subdivided into smaller neighborhoods. Forms interact with light to shape space, creating a well-defined sense of place in which the firm's fundamental principle is reflected – that architecture needs to connect with people.

The design team capitalized on the high ceiling, leaving it exposed throughout much of the office. A dropped ceiling plane defines an interior corridor, guiding visitors past large photographs that slide along concealed tracks to cover storage cabinets. Guests are also exposed to a laboratory of design – color, hardware, lighting, furnishings, and techniques for creating rooms within a voluminous space. Circular and elliptical cutouts in the ceiling plane reveal colorful uplit coves that add

date of completion	2002
number of employees	70
total square footage	22,769
number of conference rooms	7
typical workspace	65 sf

Photography Credit:
Nick Merrick
Hedrich Blessing

4

3

distinction to conference rooms and a sense of playfulness to the office. An open-plan layout for workstations, enhanced by the high, exposed ceiling, was employed to create a more collaborative work environment. Regardless of role in the firm, all staff members work side-by-side in fully mobile workstations, equipped with maple tabletops on castered, powder-coated steel legs, industrial chrome wire shelving, and Homasote panels with aluminum framing and hardware. Workstations are 100% flexible as a result of the castered furnishings and floor-mounted electrical, voice and data controls. Seven conference rooms of varying sizes are placed throughout the office to facilitate staff and client meetings. The office plan is designed to accommodate future expansion into the remaining 20% of the floor plate, with no disruption to existing space during construction. Current infrastructure also includes video conferencing and wireless technology.

8

A major consideration in the office design was the sustainability of our resources — from the selection of the materials, of which the interior was to be constructed or the energy spent in the process of producing the materials, to the energy that would be consumed to operate the office through time. Recycled workstation panels were selected in lieu of traditional systems. Homosote 440 tack panels, made from 100% post-consumer recycled newsprint, were mechanically fastened to unpainted conference room walls, utilizing no adhesives to affect indoor air quality. These wall panels will be completely recyclable in the future. The carpet is also recyclable. A high-efficiency halogen lighting system, operated by motion sensors, responds to the need for changing light levels and energy efficiency. Easy-to-adjust window shades reduce window heat gain, as needed. No endangered wood species were used and, to reduce waste, existing furniture was reused wherever possible. In the end, creating a flexible and sustainable environment has given staff members a sense of ownership and control over their workplace that is reflected in their team spirit and the quality of their work.

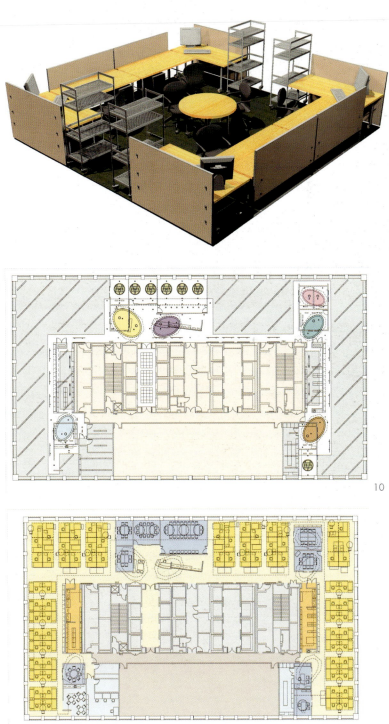

9

10

Reality of Design

the
designer's
workspace

One's environment affects one's state of mind. The designer works with typical office designs each day – workstations, lobbies, reception areas, conference rooms, etc. But, the use of these spaces by the designer on a daily basis in his or her own firm affects the reality of design. The architect, landscape architect, graphic designer and the interior designer's work environment has direct impact on work, productivity, creativity, accessibility, and morale.

The majority of the firm examples in this book reflect an open studio atmosphere. Whether the firm is small (1 to 19), medium (20 to 49), or large (50 and up), each office approach exhibits the open studio philosophy. This arrangement reflects the 'team approach.' During college, the design student will learn that only a small portion of a designer's education occurs during the university years. After graduation, the intern has the opportunity to work with a team and gain knowledge from the experienced team members. Through the years, the theories and design approaches, as learned in design labs, will be supplemented with detailing and construction experience.

Is the excitement from the university design studio comparable to that in your studio? Our educational environment taught us that critique and input from others usually enriches the final product. Does the design of the space facilitate this process? Does the layout make interaction easy? Not only do the younger, more inexperienced members of the team learn from the more experienced, they learn from each other. As design is a cyclical process, ideas are constantly polished by input from other team members. Isolation of certain team members can hinder this process. Are your project managers in the studio or separated into individual offices? Does the separation of project managers from the studio impact or hinder the team learning experience? Interns

and project architects or interior designers learn from their mentor's phone calls and daily interaction with consultants and contractors. The philosophy of a total open studio or a combination is quite varied through the case studies illustrated in this book. What works best for your firm? As your firm grows or downsizes, carefully re-evaluate where the learning curve is occurring and how your staff is working best.

The architectural and engineering sector has increased tremendously in the past six years. According to numbers published by DPIC Companies in 2002, the number of total firms in the United States has increased from 88,000 firms in 1996 to over 143,000 firms in 2001. Seventy-one percent of these firms have five or fewer employees, thirty-two percent have more than five employees, and only eight percent have more than twenty-five employees. With the 1,522,000 individuals employed in these firms, growth and change are inevitable. Where does your firm stand? Are you growing or downsizing? Are you needing more or less space? Are you renovating?

The design professional has a distinct advantage compared to other businesses when anticipating a renovation, a relocation, or a reorganization of a firm's workspace. The designer has the unique ability to see the big picture, analyze the problem, break it into parts, disassemble and reassemble to meet the needs of the client. The analysis and programming phase for a new workspace is one of the most crucial elements in the design process. Design firms have the past experience and knowledge for asking the right questions to formulate the most appropriate program. The designer also has the capabilities and resources available that provide the most innovative and applicable materials and products for the workspace.

'To create an efficient and comfortable working environment.'

Dasic Architects

. . . to create a fully open work space in the form of a 'workshop' space, where all the staff are encouraged to interact and be aware of all that is happening in the office.'

Manasc Isaac

Is your firm ready for 'OUT with the old and IN with the new'? As the design industry sees new product and system developments each year, there are also changes within each firm, resulting from personnel, management, technology, workload, morale, etc. How is your firm responding?

In the August 2002 issue of *Architectural Record*, Jane F. Kolleeny and Charles Linn, FAIA, discuss Frank Stasiowski, the president and founder of PSMJ Resources. In the article, 'Small, medium, and large: Which size is ideal for the future' his philosophy is exemplified — ''He sees a future where many offices will be virtual. Firms may have a storefront, but a physical desk for employees will be neither necessary nor desirable. 'Look for laptop size or smaller devices to become the next office.' '' This image is hard to perceive as most design studios are full, not only with drawings, correspondence, samples, and product literature, but with the facilities for the communication of design within in the firm, for clients, and for consultants. Kolleeny and Linn also address the question of what size firm each client is targeting. In many cases, a design firm has clients who ''mimic their own size and temperament. . .(or) clients will hire a (signature designer) for the 'star appeal'.''

Which one is your firm? Do you target clients who are acclimated to your size of firm or your design philosophy? Are you known for having a young, energetic and design-oriented staff? Are you known for having a well-established, experienced, and construction oriented staff or do you see your firm as a balanced combination?

These attributes affect where the future of your firm lies and ultimately how your workspaces function. Many new firms are formed through differing opinions in design philosophy or firm management. The workspaces of the young firms in this book could not be characterized by the phrase — 'We've always done it that way.' The use of color, materials, orientation, and unique detailing can portray an image of the open flow of ideas and creativity of the staff. On the opposite spectrum, a firm may be operating on the phrase — 'We've always done it that way and we are not changing now.' Is your firm still holding on to the 'old practice'? Does your office image portray this? Are you 'traditional' or 'cutting edge'?

Today's design graduates have been through four to five years of design using the latest technology. They have been exposed to a glimpse of construction and professional practice, but have focused on design. Each student has been mentored by individual faculty members in a studio atmosphere, where teaching has remained at the core of the learning experience. The students' portfolios are filled with their proud creations from various semesters/quarters, highlighting not only the designs but the capabilities of the tools from which these were created.

Throughout the firm case studies are examples of beautifully hand-rendered sketches of key design elements of an office, computer models studying form and sectional qualities, and conceptual drawings illustrating the transformation of ideas to built form.

Each of these presentation types are seen in the design studio within a firm, or within a university atmosphere on a day to day basis and exemplify the diversity within the profession. How is your firm responding to the changes in the tools of the profession as well as the changes in the upcoming designers?

As firms hire the recent graduates, noticeable differences can be seen when compared to new hires from twenty years ago. As the firm sees employees retire and the firm faces 'in with the new' employees, new workspace atmosphere may be required. The Generation Xer lives for challenge and excitement. The mentality of being dependent on job security is not reflected in this generation. For these new employees, a firm must offer professional development, responsibility, diversity, and verbal/financial encouragement. The LAZARUS group characterizes the Generation Xer as 'thinking they were born with power, unlike the boomer, who sees power coming from an external source.' In recent years, employee comfort has also begun to include exercise facilities, shower facilities, lounge areas, game rooms, and various other amenities which affect the layout of the office and associated financial stipulations.

Is your firm able to market to these students upon graduation? Have you discarded the old computers and are you allowing your employees to be the most efficient with the most up-to-date technology?

Many principals may be hesitant to purchase the needed hardware and software for the latest technology, awaiting the fool-proof statistics that, dollar to dollar, it is cost effective. With the pace of today's changing technology, the most innovative firms realize that, by the time statistics are published for a product or program, there are ten other advancements on the market.

Firm principals have a key role in understanding this concept 'out with the old and in with the new.' This principle is reflective of technology, as well as the workspace surroundings that are provided for the staff. From the research of hundreds of firm layouts, the best success stories have been given from firms that have the principals and project managers in the studio. Firm management has the responsibility of balancing the 'business' with the 'design studio.' The new graduates need the benefit of the experienced peers, but the balance occurs in the open studio when you hear, "We've never done it that way before, but let's try it."

Large firms have a more difficult time in keeping everyone in the studio than a small or medium size firm, but the key is communication. The designers who work daily in the studio can easily see the day-to-day problems, new techniques, and areas where change may need to be considered. The principal or associate who is separated from the studio environment may not see these needs. Communication is the #1 ingredient as firms grow in size to make sure, as it grows in size, that a step backward is not taken in design quality or overall morale. With the new generation, expecting eight hours of sitting in front of a computer screen is unrealistic. Flexibility is an inherent attribute for the Generation Xer. Has your firm explored the ideas from the youngest staff members?

While scanning through the array of design approaches in this book, materials and methods are diverse and impressive. Many of the renovation projects exhibit the use of exposed roof structure, alleviating the need for a ceiling system — a major cost savings. Simple floor materials of stained concrete, various wood flooring designs, and recycled flooring products are conservative and simple applications. Open ceilings allow for flexibility in lighting as designers need numerous overhead, wall wash, accent, and indirect lighting alternatives. A majority of the projects also have simple, repetitive, and elegant design details.

As turnover in staff occurs and the number of younger employees increases, the studio will change. If firms are sensitive to each staff member ... If firms are staying abreast of where the technology related to their field is headed in the future ... If firm management consistently inventories the firm to access 'out with the old, in with the new'... If your firm ...

Will your firm be appealing to these younger professionals? Where does your firm stand in communication and accessing your studio workspace and provisions?

From the hundreds of firms that were researched for this publication, many firms deemed their own workspaces as too simple, undeveloped, or in progress. Each of our firms are 'in progress' as we are transformed by society, firm size, workload, staffing, technology, and the economy. As designers, we deal with the tight budget constraints to produce the best concept and design on a daily basis with clients. In a majority of the featured firms, budget was of high priority. Three key elements of many of the designs include cost-effective materials and methods, simplicity, and flexibility.

Your firm can have the pallette to display design alternatives and concepts in your own workspace. Many clients may be apprehensive about trying a new product or a new detail without seeing its application or anaylzing its cost. When designing your own workspace, keep in mind how this project can be a learning tool, not only for the employees within your firm, but also for current and future clients who can see your creativity at work.

This creativity is also exhibited through flexibility — the definition of a design professional's day. From the mobility of the tables in the studio to the variety of schedules required by today's employees, the management of every firm has to closely monitor the past, present, and future needs of the company, its workload, its staff, and its workspace.

The location of a firm's office, the graphic image representing it, and the organization and layout of the workspace, are the key elements for the future business plan of a firm.

On the following pages are a simple checklist/guidelines for firms contemplating moving to or designing a new workspace.

Workspace Design Checklist

Distribute a questionnaire to all staff, requesting an evaluation of the current space and items for change, additions, or improvements. Listed below are sample questions to consider.

What is our firm image? Who are we? What are our clients looking for?

How has the previous space functioned – physically and inspirationally?

What spaces have/have not been adequate in size?

What furnishings and equipment are suitable for reuse in the new space? Take a detailed inventory including sizes, colors, and condition for reuse.

Who are your target clients and what image is important for those clients?

How many employees need to be accommodated in the next year? five years? ten years?

By Job Type   _____   Administrative
                     _____   Designers
                     _____   Technical

How much square footage is anticipated, including growth allocations?

Where is the best locality for the new office to target specific projects and clientele?

Is a storefront/streetscape entry preferred?

What is the project budget? How flexible is the budget? What are creative ideas for stretching the budget? What is the time schedule?

What is it about our physical environment that makes you want to work here? What do you wish we would change?

What products or product representatives should be considered for use on this project?

Is the firm organization 'developer minded' to include lease space in the office design for increased income/revenue?

Will a Contractor(s) be invited for construction of the project or will the project be a public bid? How will priority be given for the 'favorite' contractor and consultants?

What space allocations should be programmed for the following?

Reception/Lobby	Studio
Administrative Offices	Associate/Project Manager Offices
Conference/Meeting Areas	Product/Sample Library
Copy/Mailroom	Breakroom/Lounge/Recreation
File Room	Network/Communications
Staff/Work Areas	Plotting/Printing

The following questionnaire provides an extensive list of questions for each programmed space, which may help in correlating your firm image with the individual needs of each person and space(s) of which they use on a daily basis.

Reception/Lobby

What type of reception desk portrays your firm image? Millwork? Purchased?

What type and how many seats are needed in the waiting area? What is the color pallette?

What type of lighting will be used?

What accessories, artwork, and plants are needed to complete the space?

Does this area include or lead to an area of display for projects of the firm?

Administrative Offices

How many offices are needed now? in five years? in ten years?

What desk configuration works most efficiently? How many task chairs/guest chairs are needed?

What width desks are optimal?

Will the desks be a bought product or custom millwork?

How much storage is required? Lockable units? Shelves? Lateral or file cabinets?

Conference/Meeting Areas

How many types and sizes of meeting areas are needed?

What audio/visual capabilities are necessitated in each? Electric projection screen? Ceiling mounted projection equipment? Table-top conferencing capabilities?

What wiring is required for these varying audiovisual needs? (Involve your consultants early to provide adequate connections and adjacencies)

What type of tables, seating, and layout areas are appropriate? Will the seating remain consistent for the most flexibility of moving furniture from space to space for larger groups?

How will walls be utilized? hanging systems for presentation boards? dry erase boards/walls for interactive meetings? Is the entire surface tackable?

Copy/Mailroom

What program items will be included in these spaces? copier(s), fax machine(s), printer(s), individual mailboxes, office supplies. . .?

Are the copying/printing capabilities focused in one location or are multiple locations required?

How are these spaces maintained and who maintains them?

File Room

Are all files maintained in one program space? Are clerical files separate from drawing files?

How often are each of these files reviewed and purged?

How much growth can be anticipated for file storage?

For large quantities of storage, are typical filing cabinets or laterals sufficient, or would high-density storage systems be more efficient?

Are drawing files stored in flatfiles or hanging files?

Does your firm have a standard schedule for purging active and inactive drawing files?
(i.e. from hanging active files to inactive flat files to rolled storage to only electronic copies)

Staff/Work Areas

What informal staff areas are needed for group work?

Do project teams have individual group work areas or are these shared?

Are these spaces associated with the break area/kitchen?

Studio

How many workspaces are required now? for growth?

Will all workstations be a standard size or is there a hierarchy of sizes and amenities?

Will project team(s) be defined spacially?

Will project managers and/or prinicipals be located within the studio or in separate individual offices?

What types of group collaboration or team areas will be incorporated in the studio itself?

What width(s) and length(s) of desk tops are required?

What are individual storage requirements at each space? file drawer(s)? pencil drawer(s)? drawing storage? book/magazine shelves?

How will privacy for individual workstations be achieved?

What indirect and direct lighting capabilities are necessary? Will there be a central control or are zoned or individual controls needed? Will there be a standard desk or task light?

Where will the telephones be located? a consistent location or placed individually by person?

How much tackable space will be provided at each workspace? What material/board/fabric will be used?

How will process drawings, renderings, presentation boards. etc. be displayed in the studio? Could this be a consistent design element within the studio?

Where are plotter(s) and printer(s) located — in the studio or in a separate designated space? Do any positions require individual printing capabilities?

Where will wire management be incorporated? Where and what number of electrical and communication outlets are required?

Associate/Project Manager Offices (if provided)

What size offices are needed? Do sizes increase with seniority?

Will these offices be centralized for consistent interaction with project teams or secluded for privacy?

Do the offices require total privacy with hard-surface walls or can they maintain transparent dividers?

What configuration(s) will work most efficiently for job type? L-shape, U-shape, desk with P-top, etc.?

Will small team meetings or one-on-one collaborations be facilitated in these office(s) and with what frequency? If so, what type of configuration works best? Is a small table or P-top desk an option?

What amount and type of storage is needed?

Product/Sample Library

How does your firm's process of product selection for projects occur? In what ways would you like to see that improve?

Are the product binders and samples located in the same space? How are these materials maintained?

What quantity of shelf space is needed for product binders? samples?

Does your firm rely on wall mounted displays for products such as laminate, tile, etc.? What organization can be attained with these various types and sizes?

Are color boards and samples from active or previous projects on display in this area?

Breakroom/Lounge/Recreation

What amenities would you like to provide for your staff? clients? Do they extend from interior to exterior?

Do you need a centralized location for a kitchen facility to accommodate staff needs as well as any serving needs for catering of meetings? Or are these two separate program items?

Do you want the breakroom to be a teambuilding space for the firm — a place to sit and relax for lunch, a place to read through periodicals, a place to accommodate office parties or preparation?

Network/Communications

What type of phone system, voicemail, etc. will be provided? What types of panels and racks are required for these systems?

How much space is required for computer server(s) and associated equipment for networking?

How will this space be secured and who will have access to this area?

What is the most efficient location for this space within the office?

Does your firm maintain its own website and/or ftpsite? If so, are these systems maintained within the network and communications space?

What heating and air conditioning will be required to maintain the associated equipment for this space?

Plotting/Printing

What are the current needs for plotting and printing? What equipment may be anticipated in the next five years? ten years?

Depending on the size of firm, is this a centralized area or will more than one plotting location be required?

Are lettersize printers also designated in one area or are these dispersed throughout the studio?

Are the plotting and printing area(s) incorporated with the Copy Room as previously described?

Does your firm do in-house printing or do you focus only on plotting of original drawings?

What types of storage will be provided for the varieties of rolls of paper types, ink cartridges, paper recycling bins, etc.?

Will this space also be used for cutting, trimming, and assembling drawings?

What type of layout space may be required adjacent to the plotters?

Miscellaneous Storage

What types of additional storage are required? Where will the following items be located? Projectors, easels, mounted presentation drawings, extra chairs/tables, etc.

Each of these questions may not be applicable for your firm, but these should give a broad scope of the considerations required prior to the design process. The following page gives four options for the design approach to consider upon completion of the pre-design information obtained.

Design Approach

the
designer's
workspace

What design process approach for the new space will be best for the firm's organization? Listed below are four sample approaches that may be used.

1) Lead Designer Appointed

   For smaller firms, the principal may act as the lead designer of the new offices or appoint a designer to develop a concept. This approach needs to include surveys from the entire staff of current facilities and additional needs that may be addressed within a new office. To give a sense of ownership to all employees, individual design elements of the project could be developed by other members of the staff.

2) Full Staff Planning Process

   This process would begin with a full staff charette and bubble diagramming session, to establish all programmed spacial requirements and set the most functional spacial relationships. These compiled program items and bubble diagram may be drafted by the designated designer or design team. This team would complete a variety of design concepts and images for presentation to the staff. Designs may be reviewed and selected by the principals, or by staff vote for the #1 design for further development by the team.

3) Full Staff Charrette Process/Design Competition

   This process would include a similar brainstorming session as in the Full Staff Planning Process, but, upon establishment of the program and bubble diagram, each employee would be given the opportunity to take a template of the existing space, or a square footage for a new facility and develop a conceptual plan with the established program. Each design would be presented and, either through a voting process or selection by the Firm principals, a final design concept or a combination of design concepts will be identified. The selected team members would then develop their design(s).

4) Office Component Design Competition

   This process could be used in conjunction with any of the approaches. Upon establishment of the conceptual plan layout, a list of components in the design would be established and employees would be able to develop design concepts for specific components of the project, such as the lobby, reception desk, gallery, conference room, typical workstation, etc. These ideas would be presented to the staff and design directions would be selected. Each designer of the winning components would then comprise the design team for the completion of the design development and the construction drawings.

These are only four sample approaches, but the most important element of all options is 'team approach.' Give ownership of the space to the staff. This will not only increase morale and be an overall team-building experience, but gives the most potential for a highly designed and high-profile workspace that is the 'ultimate' for your firm.

Reality – Where to Begin?

After completion of the survey of the firm and determining which design process to use, it is important to develop an Image and Growth Statement for the firm before establishing a design concept. This image and growth statement will influence the location, layout, materials and finishes of the new space.

Do you want your current firm image to change? Do your long term goals include expanding into different project types? If so, what type of image will those target clients expect? This image could be very different if you are targeting the hospitality/restaurant projects, or the educational projects, or a focus on religious architecture, for example.

Many firms stay at the forefront, keeping abreast of all the newest materials and finishes. Depending on your target audience, the image can be altered by the materials used. For the retail clients, for example, it would be very important to display the latest lighting technology, graphics and colors, as the retail industry, in many ways, set the trends. Unfortunately, the newest products and latest trends may not always be the most cost effective. But, for your firm's own use, there may be alternatives.

During our design process, we were very pleased with the product representatives from various companies who helped with cost savings measures, allowing us to use the products we had selected. As you begin the design and see opportunities for feature lighting, flooring patterns, ceiling designs, and even the use of color defining horizontal or vertical planes, make a list of the products and contact the representatives for those products. Most companies will have an architectural pricing which may accommodate your firm's budget.

Representatives from these companies may be very excited to use a new product which has not been introduced in your city. This can be a selling tool for those companies as well, since they can now advertise this application in your design firm's space. This is especially true with new carpet products, tile products, ceiling systems, and lighting elements. It has been an interesting experience to see the excitement in each of the product representatives who visit our new offices and talk about the discounts and their ability to provide the latest products to the designer. Keep all your options open and contact your representatives early to obtain product literature and pricing as early in the design process as possible.

A good resource for these representatives may be derived from your local chapter of the Construction Specifications Institute, whose membership includes architects, engineers, contractors, product representatives, specifications writers, etc. Depending on the timing of your project, it would be beneficial to participate in the annual product shows, such as the CSI Show, to have hands-on access to the newest technology and products for the upcoming year.

Not only can these products allow your office to be cutting edge, but the research and contacts that your firm obtains through this process will give your firm, as well as your client, the best service in the future. The design industry participates in a collaborative process for the best construction projects. Organizations such as CSI strive to bring all facets of the design industry together, to not only produce the best drawing and specification standards, but to facilitate the contacts and joining together that produce long-term relationships.

Restoration or Adaptive Reuse

The previous checklist contains many questions and components which appear to have been incorporated into the process of many of the case studies. Firms have many decisions to make during a move and transition, one of which may include historic preservation, restoration, and/or adaptive reuse. A large number of the featured firms were involved in projects that incorporated amazing transformations of existing and/or historic structures. The following is a summary of types of structures of which the passion of the designers for restoration and adaptive reuse were exhibited –

1970's Vintage Public Library
17th Century Building in a fortified town
Industrial Buildings
1960's House Addition
Art Deco Skyscraper
1970's Passive Solar Preschool
Southern Railway Station
Warehouse Facility
Downtown Merchant Building
100 year old Wooden Drill Bit Factory
60 year old Mechanics Warehouse
Apartment/Office
Dance Hall/Community Center/Mortuary
1874 African Methodist Episcopal Church
Turn of the Century Retail Building
Historic Mill Building
1913 Drygoods Building
Old Timber Wharf
Decommissioned Catholic Church
1950's Modernist Banking Hall
Local Post Office w/ loading docks
1901 Goldsmith Department Store Building
1860 United Methodist Church
1895 Community Center
1963 Studebaker Dealership

As an artist has an eye for unique palettes or subjects to work from, many designers see opportunity and challenge in restoration and adaptive reuse projects. Many of the case studies which are included have special meaning to the communities and cities of which they are a part, one being the church.

A few of the featured firms chose unique church facilities as the pallette of design for their new workspace. Each of the church's congregations have spent many hours in these buildings teaching, preaching, and ministering to their communities. Now these structures hold the design studios that may study, program, and design facilities to best accommodate the ministries of various church and civic organizations. As these spaces were once classrooms and worship centers, while now reconfigured and contemporized, these spaces remain a living classroom of design ideas for the future, adding to the history of the original building. These spaces, which once inspired worship, can transform to inspire design.

'Downtown Revitalization' are two key words that are found frequently in many local newspapers and on the agendas of many town and city governments. The design community has begun to step forward, along with property owners and developers, to see the tremendous potential and beauty that the old downtown atmospheres hold. Due to a variety of circumstances, many downtown streets may feature empty and abandoned storefronts. The entrepreneurial design firm may access these types of structures and see the potential of an innovative storefront for the firm, as well as the potential of additional space for a lease tenant. This avenue can help to defray part of the cost as well as foster additional businesses or residences in the downtown area.

Other firms have seen the opportunity to pair with a developer in restoring larger structures, in which the design firm may be responsible for the design of the restoration of the entire building and also may maintain the firm's desired location and image within the building. The scope can be as small or as large as the designer's entrepreneurial eyes can envision. Where does your firm stand?

Many of the featured firms have chosen to restore other types of structures, which include retail, industrial, warehouse, or mill facilities. These elements of the early 1900's provide large, open expanse space and, in many cases, feature old interior brick walls, exposed roof structure, or wooden floors. These elements provide a wonderful pallette for a designer to use contemporary lighting suspended from an exposed ceiling, refurbished original wood flooring, and feature walls of original brick or plaster.

Restoration, adaptive reuse, and renovation projects provide the designer with the opportunity to have an office which showcases the firm's flexibility and ability to transform existing facilities, while also fostering promotion of growth within downtown revitalization districts. These projects also give invaluable experience to the firm in gaining knowledge of existing construction of previous eras, learning more of the process of permitting for renovation, assessing tax credit opportunities, and instituting the process of the placing of a building on the National Register of Historic Places.

While only a small cross-section of firms around the world are showcased in this publication, the variety of restorations illustrate the potential and creativity of the designer. If your firm is analyzing the potential of relocating and searching for that perfect location with the perfect image, keep an open mind and open ear. Whether it be a downtown loft, an old post office, a car dealership, or a mortuary, explore the options – the potential, the history. Join the efforts of downtown revitalization and make history by bringing life back to those buildings and spaces which have run the first full course of their life cycle. Restoration projects can often bring grand publicity to your firm, as well as foster new projects or clients in the area who may have been searching for that perfect designer to transform other historic structures. Think Revitalization!

'I believe in fate! I had only wanted to buy a building in Santa Monica, California near my home (I have since moved to Venice, CA). My realtor, after showing me numerous high-priced buildings in Santa Monica, decided to show me a long shot in Culver City, a 15-minute drive away. It was a boarded up, defunct mortuary. When I went inside, it was spooky with small dark rooms, t-bar ceilings and shag carpeting. A visit to the attic revealed long span trusses. Under the shag was a well-preserved wood floor. I knew at once the building had a past life. The feeling was confirmed with a trip to the local library and a history book that told the story of the Culver City Dance Hall built in 1917. Today our renovated space, with its large singular space, reflects our Studio Culture of an atelier with a common vision. Our designs now dance on the historic maple floor.'

Stephen Ehrlich

Interior Design

the designer's workspace

Working from the inside out or the outside in? That is the question for every designer. Whether it is the decision for restoration, adaptive reuse or new construction, two disciplines of design are brought together – interior design and architecture.

The examples in this book showcase designer workspaces of the architect, the interior designer, the landscape architect, and the graphic designer. While each of these disciplines may not have been included on each of the projects, there are unique parallels in the workspaces of each discipline.

Architects and interior designers work together on a daily basis, as a project is transformed from a bubble diagram of spaces to a completed and furnished project. The interior designer provides the correlation of interior finishes, colors, materials, and accessories that finalize the image for a designer's office.

Many offices include both architecture and interior design services. The differences in these workspaces remain primarily in the product and sample libraries. While the library of an architect may include a selection of carpet, paint, vinyl wallcoverings, etc., the interior design library may have extensive selections of each of these products, in addition to fabrics, furniture, accessories, etc.

An interior designer's office has to be extremely flexible, as clients may range from the very traditional to the hard-core contemporary client. Can the design of your workspace portray an image that draws the attention of both types of clients?

The answer to this question may be yes and has numerous ways of being achieved. The marketing literature and project displays within the firm can show the breadth of capabilities of the designers. What is your main target market? What image do you want for your individualized space?

The answers to these two questions will set the ground work for what the space will become. What place do the different examples of period furniture take in your workspace? One firm has chosen to make these pieces of furniture 'living works of art', becoming the accessories within the office.

In addition to furniture, the interior designer brings a breadth of knowledge and understanding of light, color, and composition which is reflective in wall treatments.

... product samples throughout the office ... become living works of art for all projects.'
Babey Moulton Jue & Booth

A wall is a blank pallette for the designer. Using color, texture, depth perception, and applying elements of interest, the designer gives life to an interior space.

Are you daring and courageous? reserved and traditional? a combination? How do you bring your passion for interior design to life for your clients?

The featured firms throughout share various approaches to interior design. Will you make a statement through the architecture and color or will you build a blank pallette in order to display art, furniture, etc.?

Landscape Architecture

Incorporating: *'a playful reflection of landscape architectural elements . . . and an emphasis on the view of Lake Union.'*

The Berger Partnership, P.S.

Convey character through rich materials that refer to nature through color, texture, and shape.'

LandDesign

How does one bring the outside in? Who better to ask than the landscape architect? Various examples throughout the case studies include the workspaces of the landscape architect.

In contrast to the architect, the landscape architect's projects begin at the edge of the building facade and focus out to the landscape with site planning, planting, irrigation, lighting, etc. The landscape architect also typically focuses on projects of larger scale than one building or interior. How can attributes such as these be translated into the landscape architectural image of an office workspace?

The landscape architect has the ability to focus on the larger masterplanning aspect of a project. This can be very advantageous for the firm who is choosing a new location. Views into the landscape, incorporation of courtyards or water features, the roof garden, the use of landscape materials for interior elements . . . Each of these are not just ideas but are exemplified in actual case studies.

Whether your firm is searching for a downtown streetfront location, a rural studio, or in a highrise, the landscape architect understands the psychological effects that the landscape has on an individual.

As the connection to the exterior is important for the landscape architect, many of these design professionals spend a large amount of their time in the interior of an office environment. While the program requirements for a landscape architect's office are similar to that of an architect, interior designer or graphic designer, there are a few characteristics that initiate crucial design decisions.

In contrast to the other design disciplines, the landscape architect may not easily relate their image to the client through the interior of their space. This challenge may be overcome by the way current and past projects are displayed for client viewing. Graphic displays of projects and awards may become a prominent design element of the firm's workspace.

Landscape architectural drawings can also become much larger than the typical drawing sizes. How are these displayed, produced, or stored? Conference rooms, offices, and layout areas need to be carefully planned to accommodate the most diverse range of paper sizes. The public areas can become a transformed landscape with light, color, texture, views, and connections.

The product and sample libraries may also be affected as the landscape architect specifies and receives many large and heavy components through the shop drawing process. Whether it may be selection of granite pavers or a prototypical streetlight, display and storage ability of these items must be incorporated into the program.

While working with your staff on the design concept, what vision of connection to the outdoors will be revealed? Whether it be the minimalist approach of interior plants within the lobby, or the inclusion of a landscape courtyard for outdoor meetings, how far will your firm's image of dedication to the landscape be extended?

To Do Or Not To Do

Designers are in a profession that is constantly changing as well as one that requires flexibility. The designer learns from predecessors and peers on a daily basis as their experience increases. If your firm is anticipating a move, the following information will give an insight from those who have been through this process. Each of the firms were asked the following questions – *What is one thing you would change about the process your firm used? Did you increase morale during the move? What things initiated more excitement and improved morale?* Following are various quotes, suggestions, and words of insight to 'learn from our past' and 'improve in the future.'

'The process...became too hurried and uncontrolled as construction morphed into move-in.'

'Morale did improve thereafter with the change from spec office space to expansive interiors that could never be feasibly replicated today.'

Bullock Smith and Partners

'...Because the design and construction documents period was so short (6 weeks), the main designer established a direction with a series of sketches and then distributed the design work to a number of designers in the office. The partner basically retained the role of editor...Each designer was given a significant area or element to develop – the main stair, conference room, offices, etc.'

'The three partners were assigned roles as Owner, Tenant, and Architect. The partner assigned to the Owner's role concentrated on the financial success of the project...The partner assigned the role of Tenant concentrated on the needs of the architecture firm...The partner assigned the role of Architect concentrated on the design and construction of the project.'

'Public and professional response to the building has been extremely positive and has improved our staff's morale. Our roof terrace has been a big hit.'

CCD Architects

'Moving in to a new office space with everybody having more space and the latest equipment was definitely a morale boost. Amenities like comfortable lunch area, roof terrace, storage/library ... were additional boosters. The new and latest computers, printers, scanners, PDA's and other 'toys' were definitely very well appreciated.'

'Learn more about IT networking and plan better beforehand the cable routes and ways of dealing with the visual aspect of them.'

Dasic Architects

'We ended up conducting a brainstorming session with staff to assess the spirit of the project...'

'Historic preservation projects have become a very important part of the architectural profession and the value related to the quality of interior space is much more thoughtful and demanded...'

Elliott + Associates Architects

'We ran a programme of workshops for the project ... called 'launch pad'. All staff are encouraged to attend and to participate in an open and collaborative workshop.'

The #1 goal for the new space was *'to create a transparent, flexible + collaborative environment.'*

'Simply being located on one floor rather than across 2 smaller footprints made an enormous difference.'

Hassell

'We chose different people for different phases as being the in-house designer for one's own space can be a poisoned chalice.'

The #1 goal for the new space was *'to be wonderful.'*

'The practice has expanded spectacularly, and the office is a superb marketing tool.'

PTEA

'There are no private offices – all principals agreed to work within the open studio to further the collaborative goal.'

'Several staff members worked on-site with the contractor resolving problems as they arose.'

TRO

Our new offices *'gave us increased credibility. Our office continues to be one of our best marketing pieces.'*

Tuck Hinton

'Foremost, the team wanted to create a comfortable, planned space that would facilitate collaboration among staff. It was also a chance to experiment with many of ZGF's design ideas – to create an environment that would physically demonstrate how we think about design.'

Zimmer Gunsul Frasca Partnership

After The Move ...

the
designer's
workspace

Your firm is now settled into the new workspace. How will the move affect the reality of the way your firm functions, the way you market your firm, and your staff?

With the physical move, your firm may experience changes in your company goals. At this time of change, the assessment of company goals can become an important part of your firm's strategic plan. Are you looking for new talents or disciplines to enhance the services provided at your new office? Will your image expand in the community? Are you marketing the strengths of your firm that are exhibited in the final product of design in your new workspace?

After the move and potential change in graphics, the firm has the opportunity to have an impact on all of the firm's present and potential clients, consultants, city/county officials, and various others throughout the firm's realm of acquaintances. This can be expressed through the following ways —

> Address Change Mailer/Postcard
> Company Newsletter
> Press Releases
> > Local Newspapers
> > AIA/ASLA/CSI/ASID, etc.
> > Website
> Open House
> Office Tours
> Website

Each firm will have a specific list to contact for celebration of the new workspace. In addition to the mailer/postcard, many firms have seen the benefit of a company newsletter, which may occur on a quarterly, bi-annual, or annual basis. After the move, this may become a new marketing tool for your new image. Clients welcome publicity for their projects as do the designers. And, in many cases, your client base may not realize the extent of your firm's services or affiliations.

Local newspaper releases will also reach a broader base through the community. While this has normally proven not to be a large marketing tool, this will get your firm's image and changes into the business community. Local organizations, such as the Central Business Improvement District, the Chamber of Commerce, Mainstreet, the American Institute of Architects, the Construction Specifications Institute, ASLA, and others, will offer opportunities to publicize for your firm in their publications. One of the challenges for each of these organizations and the media is obtaining the knowledge that a new firm has been established, a firm has moved, or a firm has renovated. As a designer, be proactive in publicizing your firm's achievements. Many city/county governmental bodies and professional organzations also have award programs for new business developments and new/renovated construction projects. If your firm has used new and innovative materials or systems, your firm may be a candidate for use in the product literature for those products. Explore each of these opportunities to showcase your 'ultimate' office.

With the new image, additional marketing opportunities may become available. The local professional organizations in the area will normally welcome the opportunity for invited tours of recently completed projects. Design schools at most universities will also welcome opportunities to see current works by designers. The graduating class at each of these schools will also be influenced by the firms who provide the ultimate workspace and working environment.

Local organizations also frequently use local firm's meeting areas for monthly board meetings or special events. As designers, we offer services to our clients and the community. Is your firm portraying an image of client service and pride in your firm's projects, including your daily work environment?

As many firms have a written record of each of the organizations or affiliations that each of your staff are involved, have you explored the potential marketing opportunities through these avenues? With the new location and image, this is a perfect opportunity to publicize your firm. Poll the staff and allow them to be involved in advertising for your firm. Encourage your staff to use company letterhead when sending correspondence for volunteer organizations. This will get your firm's logo, the services you offer, and the image of your company's support of staff activities into the public eye in ways that may not be achieved through the mass mailing of postcards for your address change.

As design professionals, we are in a very service oriented and visual business. In many firms, the clientbase is very diverse. A firm may be involved with a governmental, educational, civic, retail, hospitality and recreational project at the same time. As each of these project programs are different, so are the clients and their expectations behind each of these projects. The company newsletter or some type of similar media will be important for each of these clients to publicize your firm's internal changes and capabilities of design. Also, displaying the images of your own firm's new workspace, along with your current projects in media form, give a positive sense of growth and teamwork throughout the business community.

Are you stretching the envelope of marketing with your ultimate workspace? With your new offices, spend the time to rethink a profile of your firm. The following is an outline for a profile which can be a basis for firm growth and achievement.

OFFICE PROFILE

1)   Office Location/Contact Information

2)   Services/Disciplines

3)   Staffing

4)   Clients

5)   Projects

6)   Awards

7)   Firm Strengths

The 'Ultimate Office' markets the team. While being a hard project type to define, the designer's workspace is not just an address, but a unique environment of creativity. From the diverse list of ways to market and advertise for your new location, the designer has an inherent challenge, as each new and potential client is different. From the company profile, one can see where the firm's goals are placed.

After the move and acclimation to the new workspace has begun, will there be items of change, additional furnishings to purchase, or areas of future improvement? In most instances, the answer will be 'Yes.' A design firm is constantly evolving and, as project teams and projects change, the office may transform to accommodate these needs. As always, the designer is at the forefront of fostering flexibility.

Graphics for Today's Firm

the
designer's
workspace

You can express your corporate message through the design of your building or your space, but the most common opportunity that a firm has to get their message out is through the design of something of an entirely opposite scale – the business card.

Is your firm remembered by its business card or letterhead? Does your client easily recognize your firm's graphics when flipping through the card file? Not only is the firm's image expressed in the firm's office and studio, but the firm's graphics are instrumental in placing an image in the mind of each potential client and visitor to your firm. A conscious effort must be expressed to have media that is clear and easily readable, but more importantly what graphic is used to catch the eye of the person holding that piece of information.

For the new start-up firm, or when analyzing your own firm's graphics, ask the question –

What are all the ways that the firm's name is publicized in media form?

This statement extends far beyond the typical business card. The following pages display a variety of graphic designs for the cards of the featured firms, but, from the submissions, the following items are all applicable questions to ask for your firm's image.

Is the business card one-sided or two-sided? vertical or horizontal? folded or typical size?

What is font type and size? What information is included on the card? Is it reproducible in-house or does the graphic designer hold the rights for the graphic and fonts?

How do the color(s) for your firm graphic allow your firm's card to be most impressive? Is the graphic the only color on the card? Is the back of the card a solid color to enforce the firm's colors?

Does the card have graphic indentations or perforations?

Do the firm principals have a different card design than the staff?

In addition to the business card, firms use the following media to distribute the firm's image –

Logo Size and Location in the Office Entry and Reception
Letterhead (First Page and Second Page)
Transmittal/Fax Transmittal Forms
Envelopes/Labels
Memorandum
Notepads
Marketing Brochures/Folders/Envelopes
Holiday Cards/Calendars
Email Graphics as Electronic Business Cards/Website
Project Signs
Pens/Pencils/Portfolios
Telephone Book Ad
Drawing Title Block

The most impressive and memorable impressions are many times not in the actual letters or transmittals but in the packaging and arrangement of the paper products. Unique paper clips, the placement of business cards, personalized note cards, paper pallette, etc. are all simple ways to make your firm's image more impressive.

It is not 'just' a business card, 'just' a lobby, or 'just' a studio. Designers can have the chance to graphically and physically display their 'ultimate' office through every detail. Has your firm achieved this goal? Do your employees, your printed materials, and your physical workspace portray the image as indicated in your Image and Growth Statement?

When asked if the *firm graphics changed with the move or renovation*, a variety of responses were received by the participating firms. Dasic Architects, as part of their consolidation, reworked their corporate identity and website prior to their move. This firm emphasizes their 'design restlessness' which fosters the adjustment of their firm graphics every few years. Manasc Isaac also changed their logo to reflect their move and the updating of their image.

Conversely, Bullock Smith and Partners maintained their graphic identity to emphasize 'stability and continuity' after the move.

As a move facilitates changes to your letterhead and correspondence materials regarding addresses anyway, this may be the perfect opportunity for a new graphic image if your firm decides to pursue this avenue. As the workspace design process was discussed, a similar approach may be applied to graphics as well. This can be a wonderful team building opportunity for a design competition and critique sessions for the new image of the firm. The employees are the ones handing out the business cards, sending the correspondence and representing the firm. Employees will be encouraged by the sense of ownership in the firm when they are involved in image decisions — increasing morale and worth for the company.

Pull out your wallet and gaze at your card. Does this small piece of paper project the same message that the design of your space conveys? The following pages include cards from firms featured in this book. What message do they communicate?

Conclusion

the
designer's
workspace

The Designer's Workspace — this phrase encompasses a wide range of topics. Whether it be for the architect, the landscape architect, the interior designer, or the graphic designer, 'ultimate office design' extends far beyond the design of the actual office space. From the initial programming for a new office space, to the final construction and move-in, to the first marketing call with the new firm's image and business card, a design firm has an inherent challenge.

The designer's workspace is a unique design problem which must address a large variety of issues; physical, emotional, and spiritual. The designer must be able to reach within and touch that spark of creativity to apply to various problems and needs of his/her client. The design of the spaces that facilitate this creative process can contribute in a vital way to the quality of the product and the satisfaction of the designer. The designer's workspace is the place where the communication occurs between the client, designer, support staff, consultant, product representative, and production team.

The workspace projects the image of the design team and the firm. It communicates the values of the firm to the employees and to its visitors and to the community in which it is a part.

Many firms are very sensitive in maintaining a design style, character and reputation within the design community, of which they are a part. This publication includes firms from around the United States, Australia, Japan, Spain, and various other countries. Although cultures and design approaches vary, the featured firms reveal that designers have an extraordinary opportunity to build a strong firm image, impressive staff morale, and improved efficiency and productivity by providing the efficient and inspiring office environment. The designer's office is not a typical office project, and there is no 'ultimate office design' for all. Every firm is unique and has an 'ultimate office design' that comes from within the firm and its personality, staff, culture, and target clientele.

Do you have a Designer's Workspace or would you consider your firm to have an ordinary, functional space that lacks image? Through the examples in this research project, I have obtained an enhanced respect for firm diversity and the importance that a firm is more than an office and a workspace. It is the people in a firm who operate daily to give the firm its image and character. These individuals can make the office be an ultimate office. Whether it be the office canoe, the basketball hoop, the climbing wall, the gourmet kitchen, a reflecting pool, a prairie view, a roof deck . . . what makes your designer's workspace 'ultimate?'

Look past the walls, the budget, and any lost battles through the design process. As Robert Mitchell, the branch manager of MCI Boston Rally Center, elaborates in 'New Workplaces for New Workstyles' – ''... 30 percent of the employees will be upset before the move, 30 percent will be upset during the move, and 30 percent will be upset after the move.'' Many designers have strong personalities which seem unshakable and would probably add the 30 + 30 + 30 to the the ninety-percent who will be upset at some point in the design process. We, as the designers, can change this statistic. Keep the users of the space at the forefront of the design concept and see the ten percent grow into a 100% ultimate office design for your designers. Regardless of the regional culture of which your firm may be located within, concentrate on the culture within your firm itself. Promote your firm's image through a firm's most valuable asset – the staff.

Barry Alan Yoakum, AIA

byoakum@archimania.com

356 S. Main, Memphis, TN 38103
901.527.3560 V . 901.527.5018 F

01 archimania
356 S. Main
Memphis, Tennessee 38103
t 901.527.3560
f 901.527.5018

02 Architects Wells Kastner Schipper
1105 Grand Ave., Suite 200
West Des Moines, Iowa 50265
t 515.327.0007
f 515.327.0077
www.a-wks.com

03 Augusto Quijano Arquitectos, S.C.P.
Calle 35 N 367 x 28 y 30
Col. Emiliano Zapata Norte
Merida, Yucatan
Mexico 97129
aquijano@sureste.com

04 Blue Sky Architecture
Helliwell + Smith
4090 Bayridge Ave
West Vancouver
British Columbia
Canada V7V 3K1
t 01 604 921 8646
f 01 604 921 0755
www.blueskyarchitecture.com

05 Randy Brown Architects
6704 Dodge Street
Omaha, Nebraska 68132
t 402.551.7097
f 402.551.2033
www.randybrownarchitects.com

06 Bullock Smith and Partners
300 9th Avenue South
Nashville, Tennessee 37203
t 615.242.1888
f 615.242.1889
www.bullocksmith.com

Dasic Architects, Inc.
Ascot
2-3-3 Nishihara
Shibuya-ku
Tokyo 151-0060
Japan

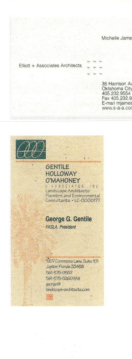

Elliott + Associates Architects
35 Harrison Avenue
Oklahoma City, Oklahoma 73104
t 405.232.9554
f 405.232.9997
www.e-a-a.com

Gentile Holloway O'Mahoney & Associates, Inc.
1907 Commerce Lane, Suite 101
Jupiter, Florida 33458
t 561.575.9557
f 561.575.5260
www.landscape-architects.com

Joyce Signs
see archimania™

Odle & Young Architects
1545 Western Avenue
Knoxville, Tennessee 37921
t 865.523.8200
f 865.523.8266

Serrao Design
690 Pennsylvania, Studio 212
San Francisco, California 94107
t 415.824.2234
f 415.824.1352

Spiral Co., Ltd.
2-26-5, Nakamachi, musashino-shi
Tokyo, 180-0006
Japan

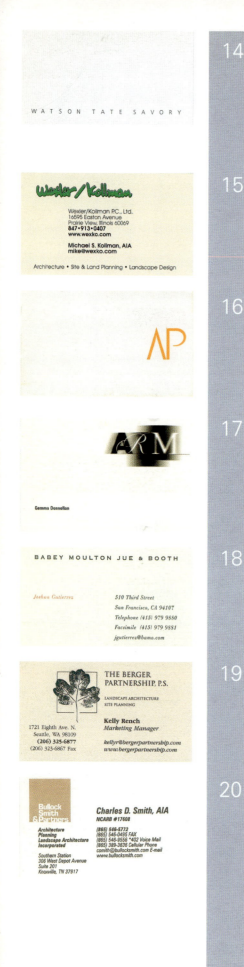

14

Watson Tate Savory Architects, Inc.
P.O. Box 8444
Columbia, South Carolina 29202
701A Lady Street
Columbia, South Carolina 29201
t 803.799.5181
f 803.799.5757
www.watsontatesavory.com

15

Wexler/Kollman P.C., Ltd.
16595 Easton Avenue
Prairie View, Illinois 60069
t 847.913.0407

16

Architecture Project
4 Sappers Street
Valletta VLT11
MALTA
t 356.2124.3981
f 356.2124.3997
www.ap.com.mt

17

ARM – Ashton Raggatt McDougall
Level 11
522 Flinders Lane
Melbourne Victoria Australia 3000
t 03 9629 1222
f 03 9629 4220
www.a-r-m.com.au

18

Babey Moulton Jue & Booth
510 Third Street
San Francisco, California 94107
t 415.979.9880
f 415.979.9881

19

The Berger Partnership, P.S.
1721 Eighth Avenue N.
Seattle, Washington 98109
t 206.325.6877
f 206.323.6867
www.bergerpartnership.com

20

Bullock Smith and Partners
Southern Station
306 West Depot Avenue
Suite 201
Knoxville, Tennessee 37917
t 865.546.5772
f 865.546.0495
www.bullocksmith.com

21

CANIZARO · CAWTHON · DAVIS
Architecture · Planning · Interior Design

John Dunaway, AIA, CSI, CCS
Architect

129 South President Street
Jackson Mississippi
39201.3605

Phone 601.948.7337
FAX 601.948.7336

22

CIVITAS

URBAN DESIGNERS
PLANNERS
LANDSCAPE ARCHITECTS

23

EDAW

EDAW INC
1809 BLAKE STREET
SUITE 200
DENVER COLORADO 80202
TEL 303 595 4522
FAX 303 595 4434

24

10865 Washington Blvd. Culver City, California 90232

T 310.838.9700   W www.s-ehrlich.com
F 310.838.9737   E inquire@s-ehrlich.com

25

EVERTON
OGLESBY
ASKEW

ARCHITECTS

GARY L. EVERTON, FAIA

400 Fourth Avenue South
Nashville, Tennessee 37201
Phone 615-242-4004
Fax 615-256-9805
Email e@eoa-architects.com

26

FREDERICK FISHER AND PARTNERS ARCHITECTS

12248 Santa Monica Boulevard LOS ANGELES CALIFORNIA 90025
310.820.6680 f 310.820.6118

27

Hans van Heeswijk architecten

Ertskade 111 1019 BB Amsterdam
t +3120 622 57 17 f +3120 623 82 84 e info@heeswijk.nl i www.heeswijk.nl

ir J.P. Rademaker

The Ritchie Organization
119 South Main St., Suite 200
Memphis, Tennessee 38103
t 901. 260.9600
f 901.521.1337
www.troarch.com

35

Tuck Hinton Architects PLC
410 Elm Street
Nashville, Tennessee 37203-4220
t 615.254.4100
f 615.254.4101
www.tuck-hinton.com

36

Witsell Evans Rasco
901 West 3rd Street
Little Rock, Arkansas 72201
t 501.374.5300

37

BNIM
Berkebile Nelson Immenschuh McDowell
106 West 14th Street
Suite 200
Kansas City, Missouri 64105
t 816.783.1500
f 816.783.1501
www.bnim.com

38

Centerbrook Architects and Planners, LLC
67 Main Street
Post Office Box 955
Centerbrook, Connecticut 06409-0955
t 860.767.0175
f 860.767.8719
www.centerbrook.com

39

D'Adda, Lorenzini, Vigorelli
see UdA

40

Flad & Associates
644 Science Drive
P.O. Box 44977
Madison, Wisconsin 53744-4977
t 608.232.2661
f 608.238.6727
www.flad.com

41

Hassell PTY LTD ABN 24 007 711 435
Level 3, 120 Edward Street
Brisbane Qld 4000 Australia
Brisbane@Hassell.com.AU
t 617 3017 5757
f 617 3017 5777

42

43   LandDesign, Inc.
223 North Graham Street
Charlotte, North Carolina 28202
t 704.333.0325
f 704.332.3246

44   Looney Ricks Kiss Architects, Inc.
175 Toyota Plaza, Suite 600
Memphis, Tennessee 38103
t 901.521.1440
f 901.525.2760

45   Marc-Michaels Interior Design, Inc.
720 West Morse Boulevard
Winter Park, Florida 32789
t 407.629.2124
f 407.629.9437
www.mark-michaels.com

46   PAVLIK Design Team
1301 East Broward Blvd.
Fort Lauderdale, Florida 33301
t 954.523.3300
f 954.524.8370
www.pavlikdesign.com

47   Pollard Thomas & Edwards Architects
Diespeker Wharf
38 Graham Street
London
N1 8JX
t 020-7336 7777
f 020-7336 0770
www.ptea.co.uk

48   RTKL Associates, Inc.
1717 Pacific Avenue
Dallas, Texas 75201-4688
t 214.871.8877
f 214.871.7023
www.rtkl.com

49   SWA
2200 Bridgeway Blvd
PO Box 5904
Sausalito, California 94966-5904
t 415.332.5100
f 415.332.0719

50   Zimmer Gunsul Frasca Partnership
515 South Flower Street, Suite 3700
Los Angeles, California 90071
t 213.617.1901
f 213.617.0047